UNCLE HENRY'S
FORD ROUGE

ONE MAN'S PERSPECTIVE

*To Kathy,
a great golfer and an
even better person
who happens to be my
Marley golf partner.
Best wishes,
Ralph*

R. L. MOORE

RLM

Uncle Henry's Ford Rouge
One Man's Perspective

©2021 R. L. Moore

print ISBN: 978-1-09837-873-8
ebook ISBN: 978-1-09837-874-5

CONTENTS

FOREWORD

By Margo Vroman

Decades ago no one imagined the Chrysler Corporation would be owned by the Germans and then the Italians, or that Japan would be the world's largest automobile manufacturer. Back then, the American auto industry seemed omnipotent – and the Americans who worked for it made a good living. The subsequent years have brought numerous challenges. Seeing these challenges over several decades through the eyes of a Ford millwright is both enlightening and inspiring. Most of us have no idea how physically and mentally demanding life in an auto factory can be.

Ralph's stories of the day-to-day challenges of keeping a massive plant running while working with all manner of people is enjoyable, amusing and, yes, educational. His description of the dangerous and challenging jobs in the Rouge River Ford facility is a must read for anyone with an affinity for the Detroit auto-industry or the life of a hard-working millwright.

PREFACE

A few months after doing a successful presentation and book signing in September of 2017, I decided it was time to sit down and start work on a second addition of this popular book. So many people were asking when I was going to add to it, I finally decided the time was right.

One important thing I learned from the first book is that the Rouge as a whole, is the star of the show. It's the main attraction. Everyone seems to want to know what it was like working in this huge, historical, complex. They were unaware of the numerous buildings that made it one of the largest automobile manufacturing complexes in the world. They also asked for more stories about the dedicated men and women, some with amazingly colorful personalities, who kept the plant operating - oftentimes under extremely difficult and hazardous conditions.

As I stated in the first edition, this project started as a result of reading a 2004 article in the Detroit Free Press about how Detroit's "blue collar" working class was fading away.

I thought, if we were all about to "fade away," I wanted to leave behind a written record of what life was like working for one of Detroit's greatest automotive facilities. And, as a youngster from Northern Michigan, it didn't take long to find out that it was totally amazing.

As a college student, before taking a permanent job with the Ford Motor Company in 1968, I gained invaluable experience working many different summer jobs for Ford. I had spent several years as an employee in Ford's summer vacation replacement program. This, combined with all the interesting buildings I worked in (fifteen) as a millwright for Ford and Rouge Steel for over twenty years, has allowed me to write a second edition about life at the famous River Rouge Complex.

The skilled tradesmen I worked with were proud to be working in the great Ford Rouge Complex, which encompassed slightly over 1,200 acres with the Rouge River flowing lazily through it. When it was built, it stood out from all the other automobile company plants because it was entirely self-contained and could completely manufacture and assemble an automobile from start to finish entirely within the plant. With parts coming in from all over the country, it was truly amazing that the Rouge was able to coordinate such efficiency. Within a few years, however, after I started my apprenticeship in 1972, big changes began to take place. This really shouldn't have been too much of a surprise, however, because many of the buildings in the complex were already 50 years old. They were definitely showing their age.

When I was hired, many of the plant's old-timers referred to "Uncle Henry" when various situations or problems arose during the course of a work day. They would look at a piece of work that had just been completed, and if it wasn't just right, they would say something such as "Uncle Henry" wouldn't like this, or, if management told them to do something they didn't want to do, "Uncle Henry" wouldn't do it this way. It was their way of acknowledging the great man who founded the company and how particular he was about how things should be done. Those old timers and their respect for Henry Ford is why I chose the title I did for this book.

ACKNOWLEDGMENTS

Special thanks to my uncle, Bill Kowalski, who was a draftsman for Ford and helped me procure my first job there. He has since passed away, but I want his family to know how much I appreciate the help he gave me.

Another thank you goes to my mom, who always kept on my butt about going back to Ford whenever I was out of college. It would have been easy for me to just hang out up north with my friends and not go back to the city to work. But I always knew she was right. There was nothing I could do up there to make the kind of money I was making at Ford.

I also want to thank our lawyer friend, Margo, who helped with editing the first edition of this book and who also helped put the finishing touches on this second edition. I also need to mention the great job that Connor Mathews did with the overall editing of this second edition.

Thanks also goes out to a pool playing friend and fellow golfer, also named Ralph, who was so kind to supply some of his great stories as a tool and die worker and committeeman at the Ford Rouge Complex.

INTRODUCTION

It was February of 1967 and I was standing in line for the third time in three years, waiting to be interviewed for a job at Ford's world-famous River Rouge Complex in Dearborn, Michigan.

The line on this particular morning, with a warm winter sun shining down on us, wasn't nearly as long as it had been the previous two years. Back then it snaked all the way out to Miller Road, and probably included a couple hundred people or more. But the last time I was here it was in May as part of Ford's famous vacation replacement program, which was designed for hiring college students during the hot summer months while permanent workers got to enjoy vacations.

This time, the line was much shorter because they were only hiring people who had previously worked for Ford and who had a reliable work record.

As I was standing there, soaking up the radiant beams of the bright sun, I couldn't help but think about which building I might be sent to work in and what type of job might be waiting for me this time. Looking back, I thank God I was able to be a part of that wonderful summer program and that I was hired as many times as I was before becoming a permanent employee in September of 1968. It was very different compared to the way things are today. Now, it's much more difficult to get a good job. My good fortune and perseverance definitely paid off.

The reason I was there in February instead of May was because after graduating from Alpena Community College, I enrolled in a bachelor's degree program at Wayne State University. After a short while, I decided Wayne State wasn't for me. So, when I found out Ford was hiring again, I got up bright and early to make sure I was one of the first job applicants in line.

Once I got inside the waiting room, I was rather apprehensive as I waited for the interviewer to call my name. My plan was to work until Fall and then transfer to Eastern Michigan University and continue toward my goal of becoming a teacher and basketball coach.

CHAPTER 1

The Old Iron Foundry

My first experience working at the Rouge was in 1965, as a nineteen-year-old, green-horned, Northern Michigan kid who had absolutely no idea what to expect from this huge complex.

Newly hired people usually got the afternoon shift, and I was no exception. My job was to work in what was known as the "knockout room," on the third floor of the old iron foundry.

On my first day on the job, the temperature outside was around ninety degrees or better. I was already beginning to question my sanity for agreeing to take this job, not that I actually had any say in the matter, as I climbed what appeared to be a never- ending set of steps that led up to the third floor.

"Oh, my God!" I thought to myself as my boss, a pleasant black man of average size, introduced himself as Pryor, took me around the work area and explained what was happening and what my responsibilities would be. "This doesn't look good." I thought. And I was so right.

The knockout room was where hot scrap iron parts from the motor castings would come down a very long conveyor belt. Our job was to knock off and break up all of the differently shaped "arms" or extensions that were left on the parts from the casting process. This was done so the parts could continue on to other conveyors without getting hung up on them. If any of the parts got caught or stuck on the conveyor line, it would cause the whole line to shut down. If parts were defective, they would be pushed off the conveyors into a chute that would send them to an area underneath where a large scrap bin was waiting to be filled up. The bins were then hauled off to one of the furnaces to be melted down again.

So, here I was a 5-foot 7-inch, 145-pound white kid from a little town up north, working with all of these big, muscular black guys. We were all swinging a slightly smaller version of a sledge hammer in an effort to break off all of these pieces of sharp metal. When the hammer wouldn't do the job, we would have to pick the part up and slam it down hard against the tough conveyor belt in an effort to break the brittle excess parts off of it. Some of these extraneous pieces were 15 inches or so long. We protected ourselves with long leather-faced gloves and special fire-proof sleeves that slid over our forearms. These weren't always enough to protect our hands and arms from hot, flying, pieces of metal.

The conveyors were moving along at a pretty good pace so there wasn't a lot of time to break off the unwanted metal. If we had trouble breaking one up, we would toss it off the belt into a pile in a corner of the room. Later on, whenever we had a bit of a slow-down, we would go back and finish removing the excess metal from those difficult parts.

Making matters even worse was the fact that there was an abundance of hot, nasty smelling sand on the belt. This sand, which contained several different chemicals such as silicone from the casting process, would cause my eyes to burn as it mixed with all the sweat dripping down off of my forehead. After a few hours of swinging the heavy hammer over a hot conveyor belt, I was soaking wet and my blue jeans had turned white in spots from all of the salt leaching out of my body.

When our lunch break finally arrived, I was totally wiped out and had to go to the bathroom and barf.

Fortunately, the guys I was working with were very understanding. They knew it was one of the hottest days of the year, which was around 95 degrees. This was tough on everyone, let alone a green-horned, newcomer.

Some of the guys let the foreman know just how sick I was, so he sent me to first-aid where they gave me some salt tablets and a strong pain reliever in an effort to bring my one-hundred-degree temperature down close to normal.

After a short rest while laying down, I was given the ok to go back to my job where I was able to finish out my shift. To the surprise of quite a few of the men, I returned the next day for more of the same. Eventually, I began feeling more comfortable with my job and my co-workers, as well as the plant in general.

As I'm writing this, I can't help but believe this was probably one of the toughest days I ever had at the Rouge. And it makes me proud that I had the courage to go back the following day, rather than just pack it in and say, "That's it. I've had it." That definitely would have been the easy thing to do, and some might say the smart thing to do. But I was a farm kid from Northern Michigan and I wasn't raised to walk away from hard work. I survived that day and many more and I'm proud of the fact that I'm able to be here writing about my thirty-three-year experience of working for Ford and Rouge Steel.

I think the one thing that really impressed me more than anything else about the Rouge facility was the enormity of the whole complex, with all of its weird shaped buildings. Big ones, small ones, short ones, and many tall ones with high smoke stacks rising up towards the clouds. That is, if you could even see the clouds with all of that pollution floating around in the air. The Blast Furnace, the Basic Oxygen Furnace (BOF), and the Iron Foundry that I was working in, were a few of the worst ones. It was absolutely amazing and not always in a good way, what with all that red sky and dark smoke, which by the way, was my motivation some years later for writing a poem entitled, "Tears of Fear."

I, however, had my hands full just familiarizing myself with the plant that I was working in at the time. So, therefore, I really did not see too much of the other buildings during my first year because the old iron foundry that I was working in ran lengthwise along Miller Road, and the rest of the complex was between Miller and Schafer Road to the west.

The men played checkers a lot while on their breaks, and I enjoyed watching them because they were so good and really knew what they were doing. I had played some checkers before, but never anything like this. They were jumping checkers all over the table and in all different directions. When one player lost, another was always waiting to take his place. It was no doubt a fun game to watch.

Most of the good card games took place downstairs in one of the lunch rooms, but because of the fact that we were so high up, the guys didn't bother to go down too often.

I also had to get to know the rest of the plant quite well because they would occasionally shut our line down and we would then have to go downstairs and work at different jobs on the main floor.

The main floor in most plants is a very busy area with a lot going on, and if you are not paying attention to your surroundings, you could easily get injured.

Compounding the problem on the main floor of this ancient building was the fact that there was an abundance of nasty dust floating around in the air from all of the sand and chemicals they used in the casting process.

There was one particular narrow passageway that was always full of that disgusting dust. As you can probably guess, just walking through it left your face all covered with the nasty stuff. Not good! Needless to say, I didn't go around there very often. It was probably because of areas, such as this, that there were not a lot of tears shed when this old dinosaur of a building was torn down in the 1970's.

Later in this book, I'll explain how I came back as a young millwright apprentice in 1973 and 1974 and was able to get my revenge by helping to tear down all of the old knockout room area's where I had worked as part of my very first job at Ford's. I'll never forget that.

So even though the work was not as hard down there as it was in the knockout room, I preferred being upstairs because we were in an area where no one bothered us.

The big shots did not want to go up to where we were working too often because there was quite a flight of stairs that had to be negotiated. That, combined with the intense heat and noise from the shakers on the second floor pretty much kept everyone else away. Probably another reason was that they very well knew there were a lot of things going on up there that they would just as soon distance their-self from.

Things such as, Friday afternoons, which were pretty wild most of the time because the guys got paid the night before and were anxious to go back and party afterwards, and believe me, they definitely were ready to party.

Most of the time on Friday's there were a couple bottles of booze being passed around early in the shift during our break and lunch period, and by the time our final break rolled around, some of the guys were dancing around the floor tooted up pretty good, making a lot of sexual gyrations. Hoorah!

On one Friday afternoon during our break, two big guys both about 6 foot 2 or 3 inches and about 225 pounds got into a pretty heated argument. They were going at it nose to nose when all of a sudden one guy pulls out a knife with about a 4-inch blade. Now these two "brothers" weren't really trouble makers, but because they had a few drinks in them, they were getting a little crazy. To make matters even worse was the fact that they were usually buddies, and both were friends of mine. So stupid, naïve me gets in between them and tries to be a peacemaker. Well, this one big guy by the name of Nate, who reminded me a lot of the Detroit Tigers slugging left fielder, Willie Horton because of his huge muscular arms, came over and yanked me out of there and said something like, "Man what you trying to do? You want to get cut? Don't ever get around these men when they're arguing, especially when the hardware comes out. You nuts or something?"

I think that little episode of him pulling me out of there kind of took the tension off and got them laughing. Within a short time, the two men had made up and went about their business. Whew! That was a very good lesson learned, and one that has helped me keep from getting involved in similar situations.

One other thing that I remember about 1965 was about our foreman sitting outside on the steps leading into our room and listening to the Detroit Tigers baseball games. They were playing some excellent, exciting, baseball in 1965 with a bunch of good young players such as McClain, Lolich, Sparma, Hiller, Stanley, Northrup and Horton blending in with veterans like Cash and Kaline, and one of the best hitting pictures for power, Earl Wilson. Three years later in 1968, they would go on to win the World Series.

It was without a doubt quite an exciting summer for me as a young kid doing this kind of work, making good money and being able to keep up with my beloved Tigers.

Another college guy by the name of John had been working in an area near me. Being the only two white dudes up there we ended up becoming very good friends, especially since we both shared a great love for large-mouth bass fishing.

One Friday night, John say's to me, "Let's go over to my folk's place in Dearborn after work and get my dad's boat and go out to Kensington and catch some bass." I had no problem with that, so after whipping up a couple sandwiches from his folk's refrigerator, we hooked up the boat and trailer and headed north toward Kensington Park, which was approximately forty miles away.

It turned out to be a nice, quiet night and we were ready to try our luck, hoping to land a couple big lunkers. We couldn't have been out there for more than twenty minutes when we saw these bright lights coming across the lake towards us. Finally, as the boat got up close to us, we could see that it was a sheriff or ranger patrol boat. He asked us what we were doing out there at that time of the morning. We just told him we thought we would come out after work and fish for some bass, and that we weren't out to cause any trouble.

He was entirely understanding and said something like, "Well, just follow me back to the landing, and next time, remember the park closes at 10 p.m."

We thanked him for the information and for not giving us a ticket and then we got out of there as quickly as we could, being thankful that we got off the "hook" with just a warning and another lesson learned.

After that little escapade, the summer faded by rather quickly, and it was time for me to return to school with loads of great memories and experiences from my first year of working at Ford Motor Company.

Unfortunately, I had to leave about a week or two before I wanted because I had become sick with the flu, which caused me to miss a couple days of work. Because of the fact that I did not have a doctor's excuse, they asked me to take my voluntary quit at that time. I knew it probably wouldn't do any good to try and talk them out of it, so I just took my medicine and waited for college to begin.

The following summer as I was sitting in the interview room waiting for my interviewer, I couldn't help but wonder if I would end up back in the foundry, somewhere else, or even be hired at all after what happened at the end of the previous year.

My fears, however, were quickly alleviated as the interviewer came in, looked at my chart and mentioned the fact that I had survived an extremely tough job my first summer at the Rouge. He said that there was an opening in the engine plant on the motor line and I could have that job, or I could go back to the foundry. He said this with a bit of a grin on his face because he knew I would be only too happy to get away from that dusty, old dinosaur of a building.

CHAPTER 2

The Dearborn Engine Plant

Every building in the Rouge Complex had its own peculiarities, and the Dearborn Engine Plant (DEP) was no exception. The first thing that I noticed in that plant was a distinctive haze of oil floating around in the air. And secondly, most of the floors in the building were made of a hard, smooth and shiny, steel plate.

One of the biggest reasons for all of the oil used in this plant was to facilitate the drilling and reaming out of all the holes in the motors. Because of this process, there were often oil spills, which caused the steel floors to be extremely slippery. Not for long, however, because there was always a large floor scrubber, which reminded me of the Zamboni ice-cleaning machine, going around the plant keeping the floors dry and clean.

I later found out that one of the main reasons for the steel floors was because of all of the many machining processes. Wood or brick floors similar to those in the Stamping Plant, caused way too much dust, which would have created huge problems in this area.

Another thing I could not help but notice on my first day of work in the DEP was the intercom system they had set up all around the plant. It seemed as though they were constantly paging someone to go to a certain area in the building, or paging someone to call so-and-so on their plant phone. I also found it rather amusing that the bosses used bicycles for transportation, that is, unless they weren't in a hurry and then they would just walk.

I can also recall bikes being used in two assembly plants. The one in the Rouge where Mustangs were fabricated and in the Wixom Plant where Lincolns were assembled. The Frame, and Tool and Die Plants in the Rouge also used them.

Later on in the 1970's, they started using little orange, three wheeled, battery powered carts that also had room for one person to ride on the back, or to carry parts. These little "scooters" were very quick, but would tip over fairly easily if the operator was to get a little careless.

And, speaking of careless, when I was working in the Stamping Plant as a millwright in the early 1980's, one of our bosses had a reputation for crashing his vehicle. Everyone knew that he was going to eventually end up hurting someone because he was always in such a big hurry (just a complete idiot.) Well, one day he was flying around a corner on his scooter and hit a woman. She was hurt, not real bad, but never the less he did hurt her. The company ended up giving him some time off, maybe a week or so. I can't remember for sure, but it probably wasn't long enough.

Another time, maybe a year or two later, this same man hit this crippled up, cribs-man who was walking down the second floor ramp to the ground floor instead of taking the stairs because he had a bad leg and therefore, it was easier for him to use the ramp. I don't know all of the details of the accident, but he hurt the guy bad enough for him to miss many weeks of work, and rather than come back, I think the old boy just retired. A few weeks after the accident, and after serving another suspension, this guy ended up getting hired as a boss in the Wixom Assembly Plant. It was truly amazing.

My assignment on the motor line was to torque down the head bolts to approximately 110-120 pounds of pressure using a long-handled torque wrench. I cannot recall exactly how many bolts we had to torque on each side of the motor, but it was something like two rows of eight or ten bolts going from top to bottom.

As fast as these motors moved along, I had my hands full that first week just trying to keep up. Occasionally, if I got behind, my partner, who was a short muscular black fellow by the name of Tom Washington, would have to bail me out. It took the two of us to do this job, and from what I remember, he did one side of the motor and I did the other.

Just as it was the year before, it was a learning and conditioning process. I had to take a lot of good- natured kidding from Tom, who was actually quite good about helping me and giving me tips on how to position the moving motor to facilitate the tightening of the bolts. When you work on an assembly line, such as the motor line, most workers have one main job that they do day in and day out, and they pretty much stick to it. However, everyone had to know how to do quite a few different jobs on the line because of absences and injuries, which were rather common on the line. In recent years, that has changed some, but for the most part, absences and injuries are still two very big problems.

After a couple of weeks, I was keeping up with the line almost as well as Tom, and not much longer after that, we were working together so well we could give each other a short break.

Speaking of breaks, I remember this one time I came back from my break maybe a minute late. The relief man we had was always trying to intimidate people by telling them that they better be back exactly on time from their break, or he would cut them short on their next one. He was a cocky, young black dude of average size, who always wore a "do-rag" around his slicked- down hair, and kind of reminded me of a pimp. Anyhow, he wasn't too happy with me coming back a little late and made some wisecrack remark about it.

Well, I wasn't about to be intimidated by someone like this, and I let him know that I wasn't the only one who came back a little late on occasion, actually some guys made this a regular habit, and I didn't hesitate to remind him of this and the fact that I was usually always back on time. He, of course, did not care for the fact that I stood up to him, and so he made some remark about meeting me in the parking lot at the end of the shift. My buddy Tom, who had been listening to all of this, got tired of his BS and told him he'd better get out of there and stop threatening people or he was going to kick his ass. Tom, who was probably an inch shorter than me and maybe 155 pounds, was both strong and fearless. From that point on we didn't have any more trouble with this guy, whose name I can no longer remember. I still can remember, however, that all he wanted to do was sit around and play a card game called "Tonk" with his buddies whenever he wasn't busy harassing people.

Tom and I both enjoyed boxing, so occasionally we would spar around during our lunch break. I always thought that I was a fairly good boxer until I met him. His hands were so quick that he would regularly knock my glasses off my face. Boxing with him just reinforced the saying that "You are never as good as you think you are – there is always someone a little bit better," or in this case a lot better.

One day, I came in and told him I had a flat tire out in the parking lot. He said, "No problem", we'll go out at lunchtime and change it. "Fortunately, I had a good spare and we were able to make the change without any problems. After I left at the end of that summer, I never saw Tom again, although the following year, while working in the DSP again, I heard that he had been drafted. I don't know what ever happened to him, but he was a very good friend who I will never forget.

During this second summer, I worked from the end of May until the second week in September, just before I was to start classes at Wayne State University.

CHAPTER 3

Return to the Engine Plant

As I mentioned earlier, my experience at Wayne State was quite forgettable, but I do have one memorable story to tell about my time there. It probably just adds another black eye to the city of Detroit, which it certainly doesn't need, but you have to remember this happened back in the Fall of 1966. I was taking a bus to school one morning and we were stopped for a traffic light somewhere near Warren and I think maybe 12th Street.

I was looking out the window on the opposite side of the bus from me, and I saw this old man walking down the street. All of a sudden, two guys came out of nowhere and attacked him. The biggest guy got him from behind in a bear hug, and the other guy in the front started pummeling him in the stomach and just about anywhere else he could hit him. Finally, the guy in the back let him drop to the sidewalk and they began kicking him senseless. Then, just as suddenly, they took off running. They didn't rob him. They just beat him to a pulp and left him lying there. The old man laid there spread out on the sidewalk where he kicked a couple times like a chicken with its head cut off, and then he just stopped. I don't know if he was dead or not, but I sure was glad I wasn't in his shoes. All of this happened in less than a minute while waiting for a traffic light to change, and not one person on that bus other than me seemed to be very upset about it. Amazing!

By February, I found myself back in line at Ford. Even though it was winter, the interviewers had a lot of people to go through so they did not waste a lot of time. The interviewer quickly introduced himself and then said something like, "Well, Mr. Moore, I see you just took a voluntary quit a few months ago and now you are back here again. You must like working at Fords. I have another temporary job opening in the DEP as a crib attendant. They also need a permanent tool chaser, so you will hire in as a crib man and they'll slowly break you in as a tool chaser."

I wasn't exactly sure of what all of that entailed, but he made it sound as though it was a choice job as he wished me good luck and said that I would be starting the following Monday.

Since the interview was on Friday, I had exactly two and a half days to prepare for another work experience in Ford Motor Company's famous Rouge Complex. I could not help but feel elated and extremely fortunate to be going back to work in a building that I was at least somewhat familiar with. I also couldn't help but think that the jobs just seemed to be getting better and better, and after everything that I went through in the Iron Foundry, I was very much looking forward to a new job.

As it turned out, the interviewer was absolutely right in his assessment of the job because this was, without a doubt, the very best job that I have ever had at Ford, other than my later millwright career.

I guess I should have given thanks for this because, most of the time, jobs were just hit or miss. Usually, you got whatever job was left on the interviewer's list. However, they could make exceptions and place you wherever they wanted as long as there was an opening at that spot, and to my good fortune, that's exactly what happened to me.

The weekend passed by quite quickly, as all I could think about was my new job. Before I knew it, Monday morning found me on the second floor of the Engine Plant handing out coveralls, gloves, and tools to fellow workers from inside a room called the "crib."

The plan was for me to break in on days, learn the crib responsibilities, and then, after a couple weeks or so, they would start showing me the areas where I had to pick up dull drills and reamers. There were mini-stations between the presses downstairs where they kept them, and the drop-off area was upstairs in the tool and die area.

The head crib man on the second floor where I was working was an average sized black man by the name of Melvin, who was probably around forty-five years old. Right away I could see that Melvin had been doing this job for quite a few years because he was very relaxed and comfortable in all aspects of it. He was extremely easy to get along with and was great at answering all of the questions I was peppering him with in an effort to learn all of the procedures up there as quickly as possible. In those days there weren't any computers, so everything had to be done with special request (requisition) cards that had to be filled out and filed.

So, thanks to Melvin, I learned my job rather quickly, which was good because than I could concentrate on the tool chasing job and making more money.

I was fortunate to meet a lot of people in the crib, and some of them were, shall I put it nicely, rather odd. I met one guy who Melvin jokingly called his girlfriend. He would come up to the window, his hair in a perm, and lay his purse down on the counter while talking like a little sissy girl. He would have his arms going in all directions and his eyes would be blinking and darting all over the place. What a hoot!

Melvin said that this guy and another one just like him would come up there just about every day or so and put on a show like that. Being new to all of this, I thought it was rather funny, but they took themselves pretty seriously, so I just played it cool and never said anything to embarrass or hurt them.

One day while getting ready to throw a pair of coveralls into a large laundry bag, I felt something in one of the pockets. After reaching in and pulling the object out I was rather surprised to find a nice high school ring.

We had no idea who might have turned those coveralls in or when, because they had been lying in a large pile for quite a while with several others. Melvin suggested we hang the ring up where everyone could easily see it. Amazing as it may seem, after a couple months or so the ring was still there and Melvin said I might as well take it because it looked like no one was going to claim it. I still have that ring today.

Finally, the bosses felt that I was fully capable of handling the crib job by myself and also start the tool-chasing job, so they transferred me to midnights. Needless to say, I was happy to have earned their trust, but I was still a bit apprehensive knowing I would be up there by myself.

My boss on midnights was a tall, slim white guy in his late 50's who, right off the bat, laid down the rules and what he expected of me. He wanted to make sure that I always answered the bell or buzzer at the crib window, whenever they rang for me. He explained that this was very important, and that he didn't mind if I read a magazine, probably a playboy because there were a whole stack of them up there, when things were a little slow, but that I had better be there when they needed me.

He was saying all of this because he did not want to hear any complaints coming back from the maintenance department that their guys were having to wait too long in line at the crib on midnights. That would not have gone over too well. I completely understood this, so I always did my best to make sure I took good care of those guys.

The first hour or two of the shift was always the busiest, and then there was a bit of a lull until the 3 pm lunchtime when a few guys would always come around for something or the other. They weren't there for long, however, because they were anxious to get on with their lunch break.

The next rush was around 5 am or 5:30 am for the day-shift guys who were working 10 hours. There was one guy, a tool and die worker, who would bring me a cup of coffee every morning around 5:30 am when he came for clean coveralls. I didn't even have to look at the clock to know what time it was, because he was always there at the exact same time every day before anyone else. I actually enjoyed seeing all these guys come in like that and how they had developed little habits over the course of their career. I definitely found this to be rather amusing.

Being a cribs man did have its perks because there was always someone coming by who wanted little favors done for them. Maybe a better pair of coveralls or shop coat, a brown colored light coat that hung down just below the waist and could be worn over coveralls or a tee shirt. Sometimes they might even want an extra pair of gloves, depending on what type of job they might have that particular day. It was no big deal and nothing I could not handle diplomatically.

One of the men who used to stop by and BS at the crib was a tall, thin millwright apprentice by the name of Glenn T. McGrew, who eventually became my millwright boss in the Dearborn Stamping Plant.

Glenn was also the central figure in a very popular poem I wrote as a millwright while working afternoons in the Stamping Plant during the mid- 1980s. The poem was titled The Stamping Plant Blues and more or less kick started my butt into writing even more poems. I ended up writing about everything from production in the DSP, to the popular Ford Mustang, to the air pollution around the plants, and the constant depression we went through when Ford was threatening to shut down the Rouge. It was all absolutely amazing!

I can hardly wait to start writing about that section of the book, as you can probably tell. It's going to be about a great, exciting time and also about how some skilled tradesmen, including myself, got stiffed by our local 600 when we transferred from Ford to Rouge Steel in 1990 after Ford sold the steel division to Carl Valdisari.

However, until then, I'll tell you more about some of the things that happened in the Engine Plant.

After my midnight shift ended as a cribs man, I worked 4 hours more nearly every day during the week as a tool chaser. One of the reasons I was able to get so many hours was because one of the tool chasers on days was a big boozer, and consequently, he was absent quite often. As a result, they were always asking me to stay over, which I was only too happy to do.

I had a little gas-powered flatbed truck that I used to transport the tools. I had to pick them up downstairs and then hustle them upstairs to be re-sharpened in the tool and die area. Then I would load up the ones that they had ready to go and distribute them to their correct areas. It was an important job that kept me on the ball because if there was any hold-up because the machinists didn't have the tools they needed; I would be the one to get chewed out. I did not want that to happen, so I was always hustling to get the tools back to them on time. It was challenging, but fun.

That summer, the Engine Plant hired three more college guys to help out in the cribs. I wish I could remember their names, but I can't. Two of these guys were assigned midnights to make things a little easier for me. They worked in the main crib downstairs, doing a lot of paper work and filling the bins with parts that came in during the day. The day and afternoon shifts were usually so busy that most of the inventory work, such as, stocking the shelves and doing paper work was left up to the midnight shift. Whenever things got a little slow upstairs, my boss would have me go downstairs and do the paperwork, but now with the new guys there it was easier for everyone.

Because I had been there a few months longer, I was the leader of the crew. We had the whole place to ourselves on midnights and we used to race the little gas trucks we used for tool chasing up and down the ramp that led from the first floor to the second. Now that I look back, it was amazing that we never wrecked anything. I guess we must have been careful enough not to lose our jobs. We also must have done a reasonably good job because our boss never bothered us too much. I think he was smart enough not to want to know what three young college kids were doing in their spare time on midnights. As long as we did what we were supposed to, he could tolerate our occasional "fooling around."

I remember one weekend while I was working the crib upstairs and my boss was one of the supervisors from days. He was a divorced guy who had been out partying and came in to work all boozed up. He had managed to make his way upstairs into the crib and found a comfortable spot on some laundry bags and fell asleep for about four hours. He felt quite a bit better after that and was able to finish the shift out and be half-way sober for when the day shift people came in.

I knew all about sleeping on those laundry bags, because I would often nap on them on the weekend during my lunch break when things got rather slow.

In fact, one Saturday night it was extremely quiet with very few men coming to the crib window and I fell asleep on those bags and did not wake up until someone rang the buzzer around 5 am!

Another crib story I have to tell is about getting into a big row with the afternoon cribs man. He was a young, black guy, probably in his late twenties and he used to leave the crib a real mess all the time. I finally got tired of cleaning up all of his junk and mentioned it to him. It didn't seem to make much difference because the place continued to look like a pig pen every-time I got up there. Rather than continue to argue with this guy I decided to let my boss handle it. He in turn, told the afternoon shift supervisor, who then got all over this guy's butt about keeping the crib clean.

Well, as you can guess, he wasn't too happy with me and made some threatening remarks, just as the relief guy did the year before when I was working the engine line. I wasn't willing to take that crap again, so I told him that if he would just keep the place half-way clean, everything would be alright. It didn't have to be perfect, but just not a mess. He mumbled something at me, but I never had any trouble from him again.

There were a lot of things going on in the Engine Plant during that summer of 1967, one of which I did not find out about until about a year later while I was working in the Dearborn Stamping Plant. Apparently, there was a big scandal in the Engine Plant about expensive, high- performance racing engines that were being smuggled out of the Rouge Complex. There were quite a few departments involved in this nifty little caper. Security, production, and material handling were involved, to name a few. It turned out that one of the leaders of this daring theft operation was a boss I knew who ran the crib on days.

I never learned the exact details about all of this, so I cannot elaborate too much, except to say that it was basically someone from security who allowed the motors to be smuggled out of the plant in huge paneled trucks.

Without a doubt, there were some heads that rolled over that inside job, and criminal charges were filed as well. In a complex as large as the Rouge, it was not unusual for all kinds of underhanded things to be going on. Just look at Ed Martin, the electrician and bookmaker who worked in the DEP and was the central figure in regards to giving huge sums of money as a temporary loan to former University of Michigan basketball players, such as Chris Webber and Robert "Tractor" Traylor. Unlike some of the other players Traylor actually paid back all of the money he was given by Martin.

After I became a millwright. I knew of Ed Martin and another bookie, both of whom used to carry thousands of dollars on them and always seemed to have one or two "lieutenants" all over the Rouge who collected money for them from each plant. Obviously, in a complex as huge as this, it was an extremely profitable business. In fact, it was so profitable that the FBI accused him of running an illegal gaming business. Plus, they were aware that he was giving huge sums of money to these players and thought that he might be trying to fix some of these college games. However, after thoroughly checking every detail in regards to this they concluded he was only trying to help the players and that was it – nothing else.

The workers could bet on either the numbers or the sports betting, which I occasionally did. I could play either points, wins, or a combination of the two. It actually was rather exciting and fun to try and figure out the point spread and see if you could beat it. It was no wonder Ed Martin was able to pay hundreds of thousands of dollars to these players. He was like the "Godfather of Gambling" in the Rouge.

So obviously, there were a lot of things happening in the Engine Plant at this time other than just fabricating engines. And, nothing was bigger or had more impact on a twenty-two- year old white kid from Northern Michigan than the famous Detroit race riot in the summer of 1967.

I can still remember seeing police cars in the Northwest Detroit area near Joy Road and the Southfield Freeway service drive going by with their windows down and sawed off twelve-gauge shotguns protruding out of them. On the way into work in Dearborn near Michigan Avenue and Schaefer, police cars could also be seen with their shotguns ready. It was an absolutely frightening experience that really amazed me. I got the hell out of those areas as quickly as I possibly could whenever I saw those cars drive by.

I can also remember sitting around the plant talking with some of the black guys about everything that was happening. Some of them lived not too far from the areas that were hit the hardest and had to drive by places that were burning down and continued to smolder for up to a week or more. They said that it looked like a war zone. Whole blocks were wiped out and left with nothing but a bunch of charred buildings and broken glass spread out all over the place.

There were, as far as I know, never any altercations in the plant as a result of what was happening on the outside. Inside the plant, we were all brothers, working side by side, doing our jobs and getting along with each other. We discussed how very sad it was that something like that had to happen. There were a lot of old, dilapidated buildings in some of those areas that probably needed to be torched, but that was still no excuse for burning down everything in sight.

That was, without a doubt, the one thing that stood out during my seven-month term in the Engine Plant. After the riots, everything else seemed secondary. The summer seemed to go by too fast, and before I knew it, I was preparing to take my third voluntary quit in September.

Looking back at my situation, I should never have quit that great job I had in the Engine Plant. I was always able to continue working if I wanted to, that's what was so amazing. I could have stayed there and worked my good job as a crib man or tool chaser, either one, and taken a couple classes at a time. However, Uncle Sam wouldn't go for that. I had to carry a certain amount of hours to be considered a full-time student or else he would come calling.

CHAPTER 4

The Beginning of a Career

I ended up commuting back and forth to Eastern Michigan University from my Mom's house in Detroit. The car I was driving at the time eventually broke down. It was going to take a couple of weeks to get it repaired, so I ended up dropping out of Eastern and, because it was during the Vietnam era and Uncle Sam was hot after me, I just decided to enlist in the U.S. Navy because I always liked the water and wanted to sail.

I entered the service at the end of January 1968, and six months later, I found myself back home with an honorable discharge because of erroneous enlistment, which meant they should never have passed me when I went for my physical.

They were going through men so fast that they didn't take a lot of time to thoroughly check them all out. So, after about three weeks of bumming around after I returned, I decided to go back to Ford. Big surprise, huh?

The year 1968 was not only important in my life because it marked the beginning of my full-time career at Ford, but it was also an important year to the city of Detroit.

The one thing that helped the city and brought everyone closer together more than anything else after the '67 riots was the following year when the Detroit Tigers won the World Series.

They were led by future Hall-of-Famer Al Kaline; hometown hero Willie Horton; former U of M star catcher Bill Freehan; a comical Texan who made us all laugh Storm'n Norman Cash; and a couple of great pitchers, Denny McClain and Mickey Lolich.

The team was having a great year and had the whole city of Detroit very excited, as well as the rest of the state. As a huge Tigers fan, I was definitely looking forward to going down to the ballpark and watching the boys kick butt and see if Denny could win thirty games, which he, of course, went on to do.

Even though I was going to be working production in the Stamping Plant on something called the pillar and cowl lines, and even though it did not sound too good compared to what I had given up in the Engine Plant, I was, nevertheless, happy to have a job and to be making good money once again.

So, there I was on the afternoon shift grinding welds on a pillar, a part about 18 inches long, 5 inches wide, and a couple inches deep, with a 4-inch handle-like part coming off at a 90-degree angle.

The grinder was fairly heavy, so it had to be hooked up to an overhead balancer that would pull it back up whenever I released it. It was like using a huge yo-yo. It's no wonder I have had carpal tunnel surgery on both of my hands.

As with all my past jobs, I once again had to learn most of the other jobs on this line, which had about 8 or 9 jobs in all. Actually, I had to learn jobs all over the ground floor, because our line would often have to be shut down for repairs, as most lines do, and then we would be sent into another area to work.

When I left the Stamping Plant three years later to start my millwright apprenticeship, they had whittled our line down to about seven workers. This ended up being a common occurrence throughout the 70's as automated lines and robots began to make their presence felt.

After about a year or so, they had a significant improvement on the welds of the pillars, so this meant that they did not have to be hit by the grinder any more. Even though this meant that there would be one less job, it didn't break my heart that it was gone.

Fortunately, with all of that grinding out of the way, I was able to get the job of stacking these finished parts in a long stock basket, which was a very good job. And, since I was at the end of the production line and not too far from the main control panel, I was able to learn how to operate most of the control buttons on our line, which was good for our welder fixture repairman, who maintained the line.

Quite often, he would be tied up with another line that was giving him trouble, and if I could restart our line if it stopped for one reason or another, which it often did, then we could keep on running and try to make our production limit. Our boss who wasn't always around and the repairman, both appreciated the fact that I could do this.

Once we reached that production limit, we were through for the night. This, however, did not happen too often, mainly because there were too many things that could go wrong and slow us down.

Problems occurred, such as having to wait for stock, which would only happen occasionally, and breakdowns, which on a long line like the pillar and cowl were fairly common.

This is why supervision would be happy if we made production and finished the night up a little sooner, maybe 10 to 20 minutes earlier than our normal quitting time.

Occasionally, if everything went really well and the guys were in a good working mode, we could finish up 35 to 40 minutes early, but, as I said before, that unfortunately, didn't happen very often.

On the other hand, if we were struggling and knew there was no way we could make production, we would not be in any big hurry to start the line back up whenever it stopped running.

Our breaks and lunchtime were always special because the guys would get together and play the card game Tonk at one end of a table and checkers at the other.

One of the few guys whose name I can remember was a short, stocky, black guy by the name of Brooks.

Brooks and some of the other guys used to joke around with this old, black cleanup guy by the name of Calhoun about his very young, new wife. Calhoun was a tall, thin, man who must have been well into his seventies. He was also a pretty good checkers player and would get real loud when he knew he had his opponent on the ropes ready for the knockout blow.

Anyhow, he was always bragging about his sexual prowess and how well he was taking care of this young woman, who was supposedly in her early twenties.

Amazingly, less than six months after he married her, he was dead from a heart attack. Calhoun was known to have been fairly well off, so of course, the natural response was, "She sure knew what she was doing."

The best we could all do in regards to that, was to say that we hoped he died with a big smile on his face.

A short time after I started working in the DSP, I had an accident with my car in one of the company parking lots. I was leaving the parking lot during a very nasty thunderstorm with strong winds and rain coming down in sheets.

At this particular point in time, Ford did not have anything but a bright, yellow bumper post dividing the road leading into and out of the plant and parking lot. Under these extremely severe conditions, it was very difficult to see this post, and of course, I didn't and ended up slamming into it causing about $450 worth of damage according to the bill they sent me.

I could not believe it. I wrote them a letter back stating that they didn't have any lights anywhere in that very busy area, and that they should, and that furthermore, I wasn't going to pay the bill.

I didn't threaten them with a lawsuit, but I probably should have. I guess they got the message, because within six months of that accident, they had that parking lot exit area all lit up with blinking lights and also a stop light.

At the very least, I should have had them pay for the damage to my car, but I didn't even do that. Today, I just shake my head in amazement that I let them get away without having to pay some sort of compensation. Big lesson learned!

One of my bosses while I was working production in the DSP was a tall, young black fellow by the name of Ira Newble. The reason I mention him is because there was an NBA player by the same name whom I believe was his son. I remember hearing rumors a few years before I retired that he had a son who was an up-and-coming player.

Ira did such a good job on production that he advanced up the salaried ladder quite fast. He soon became a general foreman and then a superintendent.

I was talking about him one day with a couple of my ex-production bosses, and they said one of the biggest reasons he advanced so fast was not only because he did a good job down on the floor, but because he always was able to write a good report of the day's happenings.

Being a writer, I wanted to make sure I mentioned that story, because it shows how important it is to be able to clearly relay one's thoughts down on paper.

So many of our young adults have trouble reading and writing, and I just want them to understand by this example how far they can go in their career if they can just put words down on paper that can be easily read and understood. And, speaking of being understood, since I have been on social media, I cannot believe all the people on there that are unable to write anything that makes sense. It's absolutely amazing with all the bad spelling and the lack of knowledge to put a simple sentence together.

Anyhow, speaking of those two bosses, a Stamping Plant buddy of mine by the name of Mark, and I used to stop at this little bar in northwest

Detroit near Greenfield and West Chicago on Friday night after work, and one night we ran into them.

They didn't live too far away and liked to stop by for a drink or two and a couple games of 8-ball pool, which was the same thing Mark and I were doing. I got to know them pretty well as they came in there nearly as often as we did, and so while I was still on maintenance in the DSP, I would stop by their area and BS with them every so often.

The guy who was probably more responsible for me becoming a millwright than anyone else was a little fellow whose place I took stacking the pillars. He ended up quitting and moving to Ohio to be closer to his family.

However, before he left, Dale, kept asking me, "Moore, why don't you sign up to take the apprenticeship test?"

I was rather hard-headed back in those days. My dad had also been begging me to do this. He was a millwright in the Ford Wixom Plant, where they made Lincolns, and knew this would be a good job for me. I kept hedging on doing this because I always thought that I would work just a little longer and then return to college to get my bachelor's degree.

Finally, after more prodding from this guy, I quit kidding myself about going back to school and being a coach, and decided to take the test and become a skilled tradesman.

By this time, I was off of the production line and doing material handling work. I was fortunate to get this highly desirable job because of a good work and attendance record and a good recommendation from an inspector friend called, "Heavy Hauser." Heavy was as you can probably guess, a good- sized guy who liked to talk about sports, especially boxing. I guess that was one time when it paid off to be nice to someone, because he played a big part in getting me this better job.

He ended up quitting his job at Ford and went into private business, where I'm sure he was a success. I think "Heavy" got into promoting boxing and also doing charitable work. I remember seeing an article about him quite a few years ago in one of the Detroit papers, and it sounded like he was doing ok, which I felt pretty good about.

I was only a material handler for about six months or so before I got the call to begin my apprenticeship.

However, during this time, I came into contact with a lot of different people and personalities, and dealing with them wasn't always the easiest thing to do.

One afternoon, while washing my hands in the wash room, I took my watch off and set it on top of the soap dispenser. I left it there while I went around the corner to use the urinal. I was only gone for a short time, but I guess it was long enough for this brother to grab the watch and run off with it. I knew who it was, too, because he was the only other guy in there besides myself, and I recognized him as a material handler who worked in another area of the building from where I worked.

I was upset with myself for leaving it out where it would be tempting for someone to take, and also because it was a nice Benrus watch that I had bought while in the Navy.

The following day, I was standing in the main aisle talking with a buddy of mine. This same guy comes riding by on his grip tow, a little battery powered, three-wheeled vehicle that the operator stood on, and was used for towing stock racks around. Believe it or not, this dummy was wearing my watch.

Recognizing it, I immediately yelled at him, but he didn't stop, so I proceeded to contact my foreman who then called security. I identified the watch for them before they went and apprehended the guy. When they came back with him, they asked me if I wanted to press charges. I said," No, I just want my watch back."

After that little incident, we just kind of ignored each other. Fortunately, we worked in different areas, so we did not come in contact too often.

I also remember a tall, old white foreman by the name of Tom, who could be a real asshole to material handlers. He was ok if you worked production for him, which I did a couple of times, but he was very demanding when it came to setting up the stock racks for his jobs.

Everything had to be just right for him or he would start ranting and raving, probably just trying to intimidate me because he knew I was new to the job.

I tried my best to ignore most of his crap and just do as good of a job as I could, but he would get on my nerves occasionally when he would whine to my boss if something wasn't just right.

I could only look at it as, you win some, you lose some, and you can't please everyone all the time.

As a material handler, I got to know the building a lot better because I often had jobs all over the place. Up to this point, however, I had never worked upstairs on the second floor, so I didn't really know what was going on up there.

Well, I learned real fast, because most of the time when I worked overtime on Saturdays, I was sent up there to work.

What a shock that was with all that noise from the many huge presses stamping sheet metal into parts. I had no idea it was so loud. My poem Another Fender, that I wrote while working afternoons as a millwright in the Stamping Plant, will be coming up a little later in this book and tells what it was like working on these noisy lines.

Working downstairs was altogether different because there weren't any of the big presses on this floor and therefore, not as much noise. At this time, the ground floor consisted of many small, single and double- point presses and c frame lines, which were a series of c frame presses in line with each other that transferred a part from beginning to end through a series of welds in each c frame section.

Sparks would fly out all over the place as the part was being welded. Most of these lines took anywhere from six to twelve production people to operate, while a welder fixture repairman stood by for any occasional break-downs and adjustments. He could easily start or stop the line by pushing buttons on a large electrical control panel.

Years later, when I came back into the Stamping Plant as a millwright, I learned that welder fixture repairmen were disliked by a lot of the trades-men because they did not have to go through an apprenticeship program like other tradesmen. They were looked on as non-tradesmen and most of the higher seniority tradesmen referred to them as scabs.

Welder fixture repairman was considered an upgrader job. They could put a bid in for it, and if they were lucky, they got it. Later on, they had to take a few classes for the position, but nothing close to the three- and- a- half years that millwrights, electricians, pipe fitters, and others went through. Riggers were similar to welder fixture repairmen. They were put on as upgrad-ers also. I always felt that they were kind of a luxury item to have around, because in most of the Ford plants, millwrights did their own rigging. The steel division, however, was known to have more riggers because of all of the heavier equipment that was constantly being moved around and they knew all the tricks as to how to safely do this.

Anyhow, at the end of that long line, the parts were loaded into a stock rack or basket depending on the type of part.

My responsibility as a material handler was to move them out of the way once they were full, put in a new basket or rack, and then take the loaded one to another area where a tow truck would eventually haul three or four of them off together to a train loading area. Here, a hi-lo, or fork truck driver as they are known, would load them onto a train car, where they would then be hauled off to an assembly plant.

I once replaced a tow truck driver who was on vacation for a week. I was surprised at the work involved in hooking up these heavy, loaded racks.

It was definitely harder than I thought. However, once I learned to maneuver the racks around a little, it was quite a bit easier.

One night while I was working afternoons, I was driving a tow truck near the tracks where the train cars came in to get loaded up with various parts. All of a sudden, the brakes on the truck went out. I nearly went off the cement floor and down into the pits where those trains came in. I somehow managed to swerve the truck to the side and come to a stop about a foot from the edge. Needless to say, I had to check my pants. That would have been a good three-or four -foot drop! Hoorah!

I was a material handler for only about six months or so before I received the call to begin my millwright apprenticeship in August of 1972.

I was rather skeptical as to what I was getting into at first, mainly because of the classes I had to take.

Trigonometry, geometry, drafting and electrical classes were everything that I had not been very interested in previously while I was attending Alpena Community College majoring in physical education. I can still remember seeing guys walking over to the tech building with all of their drafting equipment and thinking, "Damn, those guys must be really smart. I'm sure glad I am not taking any of those classes." And then, here I was taking the very same classes.

Algebra11 was the highest math class that I had taken in high school, so that did help me quite a bit, but I wasn't very good at drawing, and didn't know the first thing about drafting.

I have always had a lot of determination and ability to learn when I put my mind to it, and I guess that's what really helped because amazingly enough I made it through my classes alright.

I did, however, need quite a bit of help in drafting, and I found that anytime I was stumped, I could find help somewhere.

A couple of my foremen were excellent at reading prints and understanding tough drawings, and so they would explain it to me in a manner that I could understand quite clearly. Some of the other apprentice mill-wrights who had drafting classes in high school were also able to help me out, whenever I needed it, just as I had helped out some guys that had trouble with algebra.

I felt kind of sorry for some of the guys I knew who didn't have much schooling and were afraid to try out for the apprentice program, because as I said, there was always someone willing to help explain things. All you had to do was ask.

I was definitely excited about beginning a new career as a skilled trades millwright. I had a rough idea of what a millwright did, but I was still a little apprehensive.

My fears would soon be put to rest, however, as I was so involved in learning the trade at work and then in doing my school work in the evening, that I didn't have time to worry about anything else.

I could also see that everyone was very friendly, understanding and willing to help. This did a lot to alleviate my fears and help me make it through the tough times.

Now, that I look back on it all, it's without a doubt the best thing that could have happened to me, because I was never into mechanical work before, and there was a lot that I needed to learn. Things that eventually helped me turn the basement in our house in Livonia into an awesome entertainment area and then go on to help build and design a custom, passive solar house in Plymouth. It was no doubt a blessing in disguise.

The Power House and Pulverizer building in the steel division were the first buildings I worked in as a millwright. And, as with my very first job in the old iron foundry, this was to be quite an experience for a young kid to kick off his apprenticeship.

There were days where we had jobs so nasty that I had to take a couple showers and change coveralls two or three times before I went home.

Coal, was used to fire up all the furnaces for power, so naturally any work we had to do on breakdowns or just general maintenance was nearly always around coal and coal dust. This meant that it did not take too long to get really dirty. It was especially fun when we had to change bearings because of all the grease involved. Not!

We would get grease on our hands, and then the coal dust would stick to that and before we knew it, we would be all covered with greasy coal dust.

We had respirators to use to help protect us against the obvious coal dust floating around in the air, but it would still get through. Every-time we would blow our nose all that black junk would come out. Nasty!

Fortunately, most of the jobs in that area were nuts and bolts jobs in a cleaner environment.

I can also remember getting some good lay-out work on huge air ducts. This one old millwright, whose name was Kit, was extremely good at laying out sheet metal for making these ducts, and I was fortunate to be able to work with him a few times and pick up some good tips.

I was, however, so involved in just learning the basics that I wasn't able to absorb as much as I would have liked.

Our boss, Charlie Rushing, was a very knowledgeable, understanding and friendly person. He was definitely a good man for a bunch of young kids to start their maintenance career with.

I will never forget Charlie not only because he was my first millwright boss, but because he was also was one of the few bosses who ever sent me a Christmas card, which he did to all of the men who worked for him.

As an apprentice, we had a form, which was a type of report card, that the foreman had to grade every six months.

We were responsible for keeping track of the type of work that we did, because we had to have so many hours in layout, fabrication, rigging, construction, etc., and then have the foreman ok it once he saw we knew what we were doing in that area.

The time finally came for Charlie to grade our cards. There were four other apprentices besides myself – Charlie, Dave, Pat and Tony. Charlie and Pat eventually went on to become foremen, Dave was an accomplished photographer and did some work for the union. Tony and I ended up working together in the Dearborn Stamping Plant for many years, until he passed away sometime in the 90's. I went on to keep a journal detailing many of the unique experiences at Ford and Rouge Steel that I encountered throughout a thirty-three - year career, and which is now aiding me in writing this book.

I thought that I would grade out ok, but I figured Charlie would get the highest grade because he was pretty sharp and an all-A student. Well, what a surprise it was when I got the highest grade! I think it was an 88, because our foreman, Charlie, told us, "Guys, this is your first card and you have to have room for improvement." The guys really kidded me about getting the top grade. I think it was only because our boss could see that I was a hard worker and was always asking questions, trying to learn as much as I could.

So even though I knew I didn't have the natural mechanical skills that some of these guys had, I was still elated that the boss appreciated my effort.

Lunchtimes in the Power House were interesting because we would usually work through our first break and combine it with lunch to give us a longer break that would allow us to play some pinochle or checkers.

I noticed that this one black guy kept going out at lunchtime nearly every day and would come back a short time later. His nickname was the roadrunner because he made these trips over to the local party store for a small group of guys including himself. There were probably only about two millwrights in this group, along with various other tradesmen or non-skilled workers.

Needless to say, things sometimes got a little spirited, if you know what I mean. However, no-one ever got too rowdy or caused any trouble, but occasionally you could tell if one guy had a little too much.

The boss seldom came around at lunch time. I can't possibly imagine why! I'm sure he must have had a pretty good idea as to what was going on, but did not want to catch anyone doing it, unless it was someone who had been causing him some problems. But, as I said, there was seldom any trouble.

Quite a few years ago, there was an article in the paper about an old black rigger who drove a hi-lo around the area of the Power House and Pulverizer.

Evidently, he must have done an extremely good job of saving and investing his money because he donated a huge sum, I believe it was well over $100,000 to something like the Detroit Institute of Arts and Science. Because of the fact that he was a hi-lo driver and was able to get around quite a bit, it was extremely possible that he was one of Ed Martins associates who collected money for him from all of the many gamblers who were placing bets with Martin and his sports betting operation. Of course, this is only speculation. He was known to have worked a lot of overtime, so who knows for sure.

I thought it was rather interesting to see a story like that about someone who had been around a long time, that I might have either worked with or had a conversation with at one time or another, and who ended up doing very well for himself.

In the spring of 1973, I received my notice that I was being transferred to another building. Apprentices typically spent about seven months to a year in one building, and then were moved to another one in order to gain valuable experience that was so very unique to each building.

When my apprentice foreman informed me that I would be going to the old Iron Foundry, I jokingly said, "Thanks a lot."

Being the first plant that I ever worked in at Ford, I was fairly familiar with it, however, I cannot say that I was exactly thrilled to be going back there.

Actually, it wasn't to be all that bad because I was fortunate enough to be put on the midnight shift where things were a little quieter.

CHAPTER 5

Maintenance in the Iron Foundry

As far as I can remember, our millwright shop was on the second floor, where our main job was maintaining most of the many conveyors throughout the building, some of which were close to 1,000 feet long.

You can imagine the work involved when it came to replacing or repairing these 3/4 inch thick, 4- to 5-foot-wide belts. After turning the power off, we had to loosen the tension at the huge take-ups near the tail end of the belt in order to get enough slack pulled out of the belt so that we could clamp it off and then disconnect the lacings that held it together. This was done so that we could replace the torn part of the belt with a Dutchman, which was a splice, in between the two ends, or if it was too messed up, we might have to replace the whole belt, which would then become a much bigger and more time-consuming job.

In order to do a total belt change, the boss would usually put a small crew of around 4 or 5 millwrights together to work on it, and then it would often take another shift to finish it up. It all depended on when the belt went down and how difficult it was going to be to work on. Some belts were a lot easier to work on then others, simply because they were out in the open where we could get to everything.

Some of these conveyors snaked around all over the plant, even outside near the third level, and believe me, they weren't any fun to work on in zero-degree weather.

Most of the time, our boss would assign 2 millwrights and a welder to go out into the plant on smaller jobs. We would work right up until lunchtime, similar to what we did in the Power House, except that after lunch we would just do some smaller jobs around the shop because we were then on call for breakdowns, which would often happen early in the morning. Lines that were running 10 hours would usually start up around 5 am every day, and so there was no telling when we might have to go out on a "hot" job, which was a job that we had to get running as soon as possible.

The seniority millwright leader on midnights was a rough, old Armenian guy by the name of Ozzie. Ozzie was always complaining about something or the other, most notably our boss, Jay.

Jay was an elderly white guy past retirement age, who was just kind of hanging on, and this really bugged Ozzie.

It seemed like the two of them were constantly arguing about how long it should take to complete certain jobs. I think it was more ego than anything else. Neither one of them wanted to give in to the other, so consequently there was a lot more tension in our shop on midnights than there should have been.

Ozzie was rather rough on me at first, but after he saw that I was willing to listen to his instructions and didn't mind working, we got along quite well.

I knew he was close to retiring and had some health problems, so I tried to take care of him by doing most of the hard work.

That way, we were able to finish our job on time and keep our boss happy. He, like most bosses, did not like it if he had to leave a note or line-up for the day shift crew to follow up on a job that we had started, unless of course, it was an ongoing job, or a big belt job, which always took longer to finish.

The guys used to kid me about Ozzie being my future father-in-law because he had a daughter around my age who wasn't married, and Ozzie was always hinting about me dating her.

I had a girlfriend at the time, so I did not meet his daughter, but this didn't stop the guys from kidding me. It was always father-in-law this or father-in-law that.

Ozzie also happened to own an old,1966 baby blue, Ford Lincoln that he wanted to sell. It was a very nice car and he gave me an excellent deal on it so even though I had a new car, I decided to buy it and take it up north for my Uncle Ray, who was a barber at the time, and was in need of a good car.

In 1973, they were starting to dismantle many of the different areas that were not being used in the foundry, and one of them to my delight, was my old knockout room high up on the third floor.

One of our jobs while I was still on midnights was to go in there and tear down everything that was still standing.

Revenge was sure great. Approximately 8 years earlier, I was working my first day at Ford on the hottest day of the year and barfing my guts out in the john, and now here I was, a skilled trades apprentice tearing all of that apart. How fantastic is that?

We had some very interesting characters on that midnight shift besides Ozzie, and one of them was a millwright we called Alabama.

Alabama, who was probably in his mid-50's, was a slow-talking white fellow of average size with dark curly hair, who came from, you guessed it, Alabama. To be very honest, he was not much of a millwright. In fact, most of the guys figured he must have bought his journeyman's card somewhere down south and then came up here and got the Ford job, which he only had for a year or so before I started working in the foundry as an apprentice millwright.

He probably worked for a small company down there with limited experience and was just totally lost in such a huge place as the Rouge, where we had and still have some of the very best millwrights in the country.

There are always going to be a few guys like Alabama around, and as I continued on in my career, I found this to be true. However, the greatest majority of the men, especially those that were trained through Ford's apprenticeship program, where they had to train in so many different buildings to gain invaluable experience, were excellent millwrights and skilled tradesmen.

Getting back to Alabama, he came into the shop this one night wearing a rather large pair of red and white shoes that he had found at a flea market.

One of our welders, Rudy, a tall young black guy with a good sense of humor, said something like, "Oh my God, he looks like Bozo the Clown." It was so funny that we could not hold our laughter back.

Poor old Alabama was just so out of place there. I think he ended up quitting and returning to his homeland in Alabama.

I always felt kind of sorry for him, but I was too busy trying to learn the trade myself to let somebody like that bother me too much. It's kind of sad, but that's life. "The strong will survive and the weak will ..."

One other character was Bubba, a 6 foot – 3, 230-pound black guy around my age. Bubba and Rudy, our welder, were always arguing about something, and it was usually about sports, basketball in particular.

Quite often they would go downtown to Cobo Hall to watch the Detroit Pistons. (The Palace of Auburn Hills, where the Pistons eventually re-located wasn't built until a few years later.) They knew some of the NBA stars and were constantly talking about so-and-so that they went to school with and played pick-up ball with on the playgrounds of Detroit.

It seemed that they were always trying to one-up the other guy with their stories, and I just took it all in, feeling lucky to hear about some of their tales.

One Saturday night while on midnights, Bubba and I were assigned some work on a conveyor, which was kind of out of the way on the ground floor.

We worked real steady on the job and had it just about wrapped up when Bubba say's something like, "Let's take a little break. I've got some good weed. We'll fire up a fat boy and then wrap this job up and get out of here."

Since we were pretty much in a remote area of the old building, I figured it would be alright to go ahead and do it.

I wasn't exactly into that stuff, but I had smoked a couple joints before, as most guys had back in the early 70's.

As we smoked the weed, Bubba told me some stories about playing basketball with guys who were now NBA stars, and also about some of the baseball players he knew. Guys like the Detroit Tigers left-fielder, Willie Horton, who I remembered went to Northwestern High School in Detroit.

The reason that I remembered this was because I wrote a story while in my high school sociology class about Willie coming out of the Detroit ghetto and making it big with the Tigers. It must have been pretty good because I got an A for it – one of the few I was ever fortunate to get.

We finally finished BS-ing, and wrapped the job up, without any problems I might add, and headed back to our maintenance room where it was nearly time to call it a night.

I always liked Bubba and ended up working with him again in the J-9 maintenance shop after I transferred to Rouge Steel from Ford's in 1990.

Unfortunately, he ended up becoming a crack addict and was in and out of re-hab. The company always had to take him back because of the various programs that were established to try and help people like that.

He would come back and work a few months or longer and then fall off the wagon and be gone once again. At his worst, he was known to be staying in an old shack on the roof of the Rolling Mill where millwrights and welders and roofers and glaziers used to stay while they were doing work up there.

When I retired at the end of 1998, Bubba was doing quite well and had been working steady for several years or more. I wished him a lot of luck when I left and still do.

I have one last story to tell from my eleven-month stay in the iron foundry. I was scheduled to work this one weekend, which meant that I had to go in on Friday night for my Saturday. Well, that evening I was out partying and had a little too much to drink. It was getting near that time of night where I needed to leave in order to get to work on time.

As it turned out, I didn't get there until an hour after the starting time, and the guys were already on the job. I knew where they were working, so I put my coveralls on and headed down to that area.

When they saw me coming, they knew that I was in no condition to be doing anything at that time, so they sent me back up to our shop because no one was around there on that particular weekend.

I wanted to stay and help them, but they said don't worry about it, you'll be fine after lunch. It turned out that they were right. I found a nice warm spot by the radiator, and after lunch, I was ready to go.

That was the last time anything like that ever happened again, probably because I got married a year and a half later and did not want to jeopardize my job.

I can remember that whenever we were on a dangerous job in the foundry, it seemed like the conversation would often times end up being about the huge mixing machine they called the Mueller. One time, a worker accidently fell into it while it was running and was totally crushed up. So, consequently, every-time we had to do any work around that Mueller, stories about that incident would come up again and caused us to be very aware of what we were doing around it, because accidents usually happen when you least expect them.

There was also a story that I had heard about guys stealing all kinds of things by taking them across Miller Road through an overhead conveyor system that ran from the foundry across Miller and came out in or by the parking lot. This probably took place sometime in the late 60's or around 1970 or 71. I can't recall too many of the details of this daring heist, but I guess the guys doing this finally got caught and were fired.

When that old dinosaur of a building was finally razed, a tremendous amount of history, some good and some bad, went with it. Probably one of the most famous events that took place just outside the foundry was the famous, May of 1937, "Battle of the Overpass." This happened as a result of Ford's security guards led by Harry Bennett, attacking a group of UAW organizers that were led by Walter Reuther and one of his top lieutenants, Richard Frankensteen. These two were posing for a picture on the overpass with the Ford sign in the background when all of a sudden, they were viciously attacked from behind by a large number of Ford's internal security force. In this picture, Frankensteen was the guy who had his hat and coat pulled over his head, similar to what hockey players try to do with their opponents when fighting, and they were kneeing him in the chest and groin area. It was brutal. Reuther wasn't exempt from getting beaten either. He later said that he was picked up and brutally thrown down hard on the concrete. They then punched and kicked him as they dragged him over to the stairway where they pushed him all the way down two flights of stairs. And as though that wasn't enough, they punched and kicked him some more. Damn! That almost sounds like something from Big Time Wrestling, but only it was real time stuff, nothing even close to being phony.

Bennett ended up more or less denying everything and claimed that his men were provoked by Reuther and the rest of the organizers. He said that no Ford service men or plant police were involved in any way in the fight. No matter what, it was a black eye for Ford and so within a few years after this they came to a history making agreement with the UAW.

This is the gate 4 overpass across Miller Rd where the famous battle of the overpass was fought in 1937 between Walter Reuther, UAW officials, and outside goons hired by Ford to discourage union organization.

Reprinted, by permission, from *The Detroit News*. © *The Detroit News*.

This is a photo of the altercation in progress.

I spent eleven long, but interesting months in the foundry before being informed that the Basic Oxygen Furnace (BOF) was to be my next building.

According to my fellow workers in the foundry I was quite fortunate to be going into such a high-incentive building. At that time, the BOF was the highest or one of the highest incentive buildings in the Rouge. This meant that we would get a certain percentage of the profits from the amount of steel produced for that particular week. So, if they had a very good week, the incentive pay in our checks would put a nice big smile on our face, if it wasn't quite as good, the smile would just be a little smaller. No matter what, it was a win, win situation and I loved it.

CHAPTER 6

The BOF and an Eleven-Month Vacation

A fitting way to begin this chapter, I thought, would be with a poem that I wrote around 1985, while working afternoons as a millwright in the Dearborn Stamping Plant.

Around that time, I was kind of depressed with everything that was going on at work and with what was happening with our environment, what with all the negative press being written about the rapid rate at which the great rain forests of South America were being cut down.

It was in the middle of a hot summer day, and I was eating my lunch up on the crane balcony. There were some windows open for ventilation, and I had walked over to them to take a look outside, and all I could see in the distance was the red sky and dark smoke coming from the BOF and the blast furnaces.

There were regulations in place that they were and still are supposed to meet as to the pollution level coming out of their tall stacks, but way too often, it was like they could care less about regulations. The smoke would get to be a deep dark color containing a ton of pollution that contaminated the air. And, late in the evening or the early morning hours were generally the worst times for this because the nasty smoke could not be seen as easily as it could during the day.

This poem is a result of what I saw that day.

Tears of Fear

As I sit here on this lovely day, my mind keeps running astray.

I dream of the beauty of the land, the lakes and rivers and the sand.

Then I look outside and see the red sky and dark smoke, and think, this is really no joke.

My eyes begin to swell with tears, don't tell me we have no fears.

Pollution is rampant, almost everywhere we look.

If this keeps up, there won't even be a trout brook.

The air we breathe and the water we drink rely on the tree's green leaves.

If we continue to strip rain forests, and spread poisonous chemicals into the air and water,

we will have nothing left but grieves.

As I sit here on this lovely day, I wonder how long I'll be able to stay?

I must say in all fairness to the executive chairman of Ford Motor Company, William Clay Ford Jr., that I think he is very sincere about changing the Rouge around and making it more environmentally friendly, as we can see by the wonderful job that was done on the roof of the new and greatly improved assembly plant that now houses the extremely popular and best-selling Ford F-150 truck. After my wife and I took a tour of the plant as part of the Greenfied Village bus trip, all I could say was that I sure wish I had the opportunity to work in a plant as new and clean as that one. It was truly amazing.

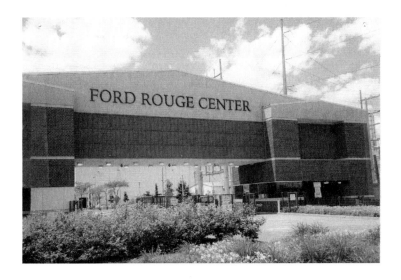

Some other things that Mr. Ford suggested to help clean up the polluted air was the planting of many more trees around the Rouge that would absorb a good deal of that pollution and then return it into the environment in the form of clean air, similar to what the grass roof on the assembly plant is now doing.

Without a doubt, he has seen that a lot of good things have been done and are still being done to make the Rouge a state-of-the-art complex.

The famous phrase, "The best laid plans of mice and men often go astray," by John Steinbeck, is one that I have often used while working as a journeyman millwright because it is so very true. And, it is a good way to sum up my short stay, approximately three months, in the BOF.

I was very happy and looking forward to working in a building where I would have a good opportunity to make a lot of money, but unfortunately, my stay, was to be a short one.

I was doing quite well in the BOF, learning a lot of new things, one of which was how to operate the huge overhead cranes, by using the remote -control box. The journeyman millwright I was working with was teaching me how to lift and transport gigantic, oxygen lances which were, as best as I can remember, around 12 to 18 inches in diameter and at least 30 feet long, and were used to add powerful blasts of oxygen to the furnace to really fire them up.

I must have been doing pretty good because this one day he comes up to me and says, "Here's the control box, take it to the upper level with you and move the hook over to the lances and I'll hook one up for you, and then you can move it over to another area, where we are going to store them."

Well, everything was going smoothly until I attempted to stop the crane a little quicker than what I should have, causing the whole crane to vibrate quite a bit, and sending a shower of graphite flakes from the rails above to come raining down on my body, covering my whole face and coveralls.

Fortunately, except for a little uncontrolled swing, the lance was alright and did not hit anything. My journeyman was downstairs laughing his guts out at my comical act, but was pleased that I was able to get the huge lance in position to lower into its new resting place without tearing the walls down.

From that day on, I always tried to be aware of all the fall-out up there, regardless of the type of job we might have had around that area, and did my best not to stir things up. Once was enough!

I can still remember this one particular day when I had to go outside with another millwright to transport a couple pieces of 6-inch by 12-foot channel iron back into the building. We were carrying it by hand, when all of a sudden, I felt this tightness in my lower back.

We immediately set the channel iron down. My partner had me stay where I was while he went inside the shop and informed our boss as to what had just happened. He then called the central medical van to come and pick me up. Once I was able to get safely inside the van, it headed in the direction of the central medical building where I would then have to wait to see a company doctor, and that's where my problems really started.

The doctor who came in to check me out was this old, white guy, whom I had seen a couple of times before since I started working at Ford in 1968. He looked to be in his mid-seventies, and from the past experiences that I had with him, I just didn't have a lot of confidence in his ability to help me.

I was in a lot of pain from sitting around for quite a long time waiting for him and once he came in and I saw who it was my pain seemed to get even worse. He proceeded to interrogate me as to what happened and so after explaining everything to him, he said, "Ok, we are going to have to take some X-rays." After examining the X-rays, he came back into the room where he proceeded to scare the hell out of me.

He said something like, "You have an area in one of your vertebras that is not fused together the way it should be, there's like a crack there. From now on, you will never be able to change another car tire again. You will have to have your wife or someone else do it for you. You are never going to be able to do any heavy lifting or very much bending over ever again. It looks like something you have had for a long time and I'm surprised that you were able to make it this far without having more trouble than you have had."

I just stood there sort of shell-shocked, thinking, "Man, this is unbelievable." I had a few problems with my back in the past, but nothing that held me down too long or kept me from coming back and doing my job. Now all of a sudden, here was this doctor telling me that I shouldn't even attempt to change a car tire if it was flat.

And, as though this wasn't enough, he completely overreacted and filled out a form that stated that I was on a permanent restriction, and that I could not do any heavy lifting or excessive bending.

He said, "Take this back to your foreman and take these pain pills and muscle relaxers for a few days." I was pretty much speechless after that and was unable to say what I would like to have said to the old coot.

After returning to the BOF, I went directly into my boss's office and showed him the form that the doctor had signed.

He was also quite surprised with the doctor's report, and since it was getting near the end of the shift, he said that he would talk to the general foreman and superintendent the next day, and that they would try to figure something out.

Well, they figured something out alright, and that was that they were sorry, but that they could not use me with those restrictions. They said that if I could get them lifted, everything would be ok, but otherwise there was nothing else that they could do for me, and that I probably should contact my apprentice committeeman and let him know what exactly happened and to see what he could possibly do for me.

Heeding their advice, I explained my situation to the committeeman, who in turn contacted the central medical office about my case. After several days of discussing it, the medical staff decided that even though my back was feeling better and I was able to move around freely without any discomfort, they were not going to change the status of my restriction. S0, it now appeared to me that I was going to be stuck with a permanent restriction because the bottom line was that they did not want me to graduate into the skilled trades with a bad back.

I eventually met with a couple of higher up committeemen, and they suggested going back to material handling to see if they had something for me.

Not too surprisingly, their remarks were pretty much a carbon copy of the maintenance people. They said that they could not use someone who had a permanent restriction, so there I was, wondering how it could all come to an end so fast.

With all of this happening, I was fortunate to have been working in the BOF at the time of the injury. This way I was getting a very nice check each week from workman's comp. However, I was still quite concerned about my future.

Finally, after several weeks of meeting with the top-level committeemen once again, they determined that the union would pay to send me downtown to see one of their big-shot lawyers.

Today, I still have most of the paperwork from those meetings, and the results of all the exams that they put me through. First, my lawyers would send me to a specialist, and then Ford would counter and send me to one of their experts.

Finally, after eleven months, both sides determined my back was strong enough to return to work. However, it was not going to be that simple. I was going to have a very important, major decision to make.

The company was offering me one of two ways to go. Either I could take $100,000 and agree to give up all my rights to ever work for Ford again, or I could go back on the apprenticeship program and start working as a millwright, effective almost immediately.

Having met my future wife in Northeast Michigan's wonderful little community of Onaway, while I was off from work all those months, and having planned a September 1975 wedding date, I felt the best thing to do for my future was to go back to work.

$100,000 was without a doubt a lot of money to turn down, especially at that time in the 1970's, but I am satisfied that I made the right decision.

CHAPTER 7

The Rolling Mill

It was definitely a relief to have all of this behind me and to start working once again as an apprentice millwright. The only disappointing thing about all of this was that I would not be going back to all of that big money in the BOF. I instead would be transferring to the Rolling Mill.

My first few weeks in the Rolling Mill, I worked with several different journeymen, doing various jobs all around the plant in an effort to help me become familiar with the many different areas in the plant, each one having special job assignments, that we had to check out as part of a regular preventive maintenance program.

In the early years, Henry Ford had set up the Rouge Complex in such a manner that they could make a complete automobile without having to go outside of the complex for parts. It was totally self-sustaining, which in today's fast paced world, with all of the many parts companies spread out all around the country, makes it seem absolutely amazing that they were able to do that. Looking back at all of that I feel that I was so very fortunate to have been a part of it. It was a big piece of American history and I'm proud to be able to say that I was a part of it.

However, very few things ever last forever and the Rouge was no exception. Around 1975 the Rolling Mill was slowly beginning to change. The company was still making some flat stock, such as, ½ inch by 2 inch,

¾ inch by 3 inch, etc., and square stock 1 ½ inch by 1 ½ inch, 2 inch by 2 inch, and some other rolled steel. But things were gradually beginning to change. They were now beginning to purchase stock similar to this from outside sources.

So even though the plant was going through many changes, I was still able to observe and be amazed at all of the many steps that it took for the steel to come out looking like that. As I previously said, I consider myself extremely fortunate to have been a part of all that history, and to have worked with so many of the old, hard-core millwrights from the early days.

One day, I had to go on a special assignment with one of those tough old millwrights. Our job was to hang a heavy 1 ½ ton chain fall, which is a type of hoisting system, from a strong piece of angle iron that was welded high up on a flat, steel wall.

We either didn't have a lift to use, or we couldn't get one into that area, so we had to use a long wooden extension ladder.

After getting the ladder set where we wanted it, the old boy looked at me, and must have seen a little apprehension, because he said, "Don't worry, you can do it. I will be holding the ladder nice and steady, just throw the chain fall over your shoulder and take it up slow and easy."

"When you get ready to hang it, make sure the chain is hanging freely out of your way, reach out carefully, and hang it up."

I looked at him, laughed and said, "Now I see why this is a special assignment." I'm standing there thinking to myself, 'Much easier said than done.'

First of all, the hook had to be about 35 to 40 feet high, and there was absolutely nothing to rest the top end of the ladder against, which meant that if the top started to slide one way or another, I had no way of stopping it. No matter how well he was holding it below, he would not have been able to prevent the long, heavy ladder, as top heavy as it was going to be, with the combined weight of me and the chain fall up there, from falling down.

After becoming a journeyman a few years later, I learned that in situations similar to that, you have to somehow get that ladder tied off and secured, so it cannot slide one way or the other. In those days, however, things weren't always done the way they were supposed to be done.

Anyhow, I psyched myself into doing it. I threw the heavy chain fall over my right shoulder and proceeded cautiously upward. About three quarters of the way, the weight of the chain fall felt like it had doubled and was starting to make that shoulder burn and ache quite a bit, so I had to stop for a few seconds and reposition it. My partner down below noticed this and started cheerleading. "That's ok, take your time." "You'll be alright, your almost there."

I felt like saying something like, "Yeah, that's easy for you to say, I'm the one up here getting shafted." However, I was just trying to concentrate on making those next few steps and getting that sucker off my shoulder and hooked up.

After finally reaching the top, I had to be very careful as I reached over with both hands to hook that bad boy up. As I said before, there was absolutely nothing up there to hang onto until I got it hanging from the hook, then I had the chain to grab if anything crazy was to happen.

You can probably imagine what a relief it was to see it dangling from that hook. I took a few seconds before starting my descent down the ladder, and then I didn't stop until my feet hit the floor.

Once that happened, I got nothing but praise from the old millwright, whose name I unfortunately cannot recall. As apprentices in the huge Rouge area, we came into contact with many different people that we were not around for a very long period of time, so that after forty years or so, it's impossible to remember all of them, except for those few that really stood out for one reason or another. Anyhow, he went around telling everyone what a great job I had done and also told the boss that he wanted me to work with him more often. That made me feel pretty good, but I wasn't sure that I would do anything like that again.

A couple of weeks later, there was an opening for a millwright on the roof of the mill. My boss asked me if I wouldn't mind going up there to work. He said that the crew that was stationed there was going to be doing some floor and window repair work and that it would be a good, learning experience for me. He also mentioned that during the summer, it would be a great job, as long as I did what they asked me to do and didn't cause any problems.

The millwrights on the roof replaced rusted out floor beams, repaired broken doors and door frames and set up multi-tears of scaffolding so they could repair the window frames for the glaziers, who would then add the glass and caulk.

I can remember safety always being a big issue up there. The floors were treacherous, causing us to be extremely careful of where we were walking at all times.

One mistake and there was no telling how far down someone might fall, so consequently the millwrights had to do a lot of floor repair along with the windows, because all of the powerful acid that was used in the process of making cold rolled steel would rise toward the roof and just lay up there and eventually rust everything out.

We would do all of the structural work on the floors, and then the roofers would come in and finish the job by laying heavy roofing paper over boards that made up the top tier of the roof, and then brush on a heavy coating of tar.

Speaking of the roofers, one old bald headed, short stocky guy by the name of Nick, "Nick the Greek", as he was called, was a little strange. He was known to spend time hunting through garbage and would often wear an old pair of shoes he found snooping around like that. One might think that he used these just for walking around on all of the tared floors. However, that wasn't necessarily always the case. He often wore them home. Amazing!

Everyone knew Nick and how strange he was, but what they didn't all know was that he had at one time in his life sung with, The Detroit

Metropolitan Opera, and after hearing him sing, I had no reason not to believe this.

Every so often, the guys would get him to show off his powerful voice up there and I'm telling you, to look at him and see the way he was, and then to hear him sing so beautifully, could bring tears to your eyes.

He had an unbelievably great voice, not only for someone working on the roof of one of Henry Ford's buildings, but for anyone, anywhere.

All I can say is that I will never forget the man and that fantastic voice, because to look at him and the way he dressed and lived, you would have thought he was a bum. What an amazing character!

My summer on the roof was definitely an interesting experience. The Millwright leader, Ed Sarah, even started growing some tomato plants in an area not too far from our little shack that we hung out in, however, it was just too hot and they didn't do very well. I guess he thought we could use them in our salad that we made nearly every day for lunch. The reason for eating all of this rabbit food was because Sarah, Jim Whitmore, one of our welders, and another guy up there had to diet for health reasons. Everyone that wanted to be a part of the salad crew would throw in a few bucks each week and then one guy would buy the necessary ingredients that we would need for the week. Not bad!

So yes, it wasn't too bad of a summer, and buy the time August rolled around, I had received my transfer papers back to my "home building," which was the first building that I started working in permanently, and that was the Stamping Plant.

However, before leaving the Rolling Mill, I had heard rumors going around about our millwright boss, and the way he was giving special treatment to certain guys.

Actually, I had noticed right from the start that there were certain men coming and going all the time, who would often disappear at the beginning of the shift and then you might or might not see them again at the end of the shift.

So, I wasn't too surprised when, a couple years later, I heard about the big scandal in the Rolling Mill involving these people.

I cannot say too much about this, because I wasn't privy to all of the details, however, it more or less centered around this boss being fired for using Ford labor, tools, and related parts to help build his go cart track out by the Irish Hills and the Michigan International Speedway.

No wonder he offered me the job up on the roof that summer. He obviously didn't want to take a chance on me picking up on what he had going on down there in the shop. However, before that summer was over, I was fairly certain something fishy was going on and as it turned out, I was right.

CHAPTER 8

The DSP Second Phase

Having acquired some experience of working midnights in the Iron Foundry, I wasn't disappointed when my transfer papers said that I would be starting at 11:30 pm. I thought it would be a good shift to familiarize myself with the maintenance aspects of the plant.

That evening I was to report to a shop area on the ground floor that wasn't too far from where I had first started working on the production line in 1968.

After meeting my foreman, a tall, medium built fellow called Rosey, he introduced me to the other millwright I would be working with.

He was a young, cocky, black guy slightly taller than myself, by the name of Robbie. Robbie, who had started his apprenticeship not too long after high school, had just graduated to journeyman status and therefore, thought he was quite a big shot.

We didn't know it at the time, of course, but this wasn't going to be the last time we would be working together as partners. We would also end up working on afternoons ten years later for the man I called the General – Glenn T. McGrew.

For now, however, we were working on production breakdowns that pertained to millwrights and most of that was making sure all of the conveyors in our area were running smoothly. Conveyors and everything that pertained to them, such as the belts, take-ups, and reducers, were always the millwright's responsibility.

Robbie and I struggled quite a bit at first to get along. Mainly because he didn't like to work and was always trying to hide from the boss. It got almost comical at times. We would be walking on our way back to the shop after a long breakdown and if he saw the boss coming, we would end up going around the back way and hide out behind the press bases until he thought the boss was out of sight.

Actually, this wasn't all that uncommon for a lot of skilled tradesmen to do because some bosses, like ours, would nit-pick workers to death with a bunch of little, insignificant jobs.

Most of the time, if we weren't working hard on breakdowns, we didn't mind doing all this stuff for him. It was just when we were really busy with breakdowns that all that other stuff, he would come up with would bother us.

After a while, Robbie and I finally started to feel more comfortable with each other. Oh, we would occasionally have some pretty heated discussions on how to do certain jobs, but for the most part, considering we were both still learning the trade, we did alright on our own.

While on midnights, I also became friends with another young, black apprentice millwright by the name of Henry Horn. Henry, who was a very cordial guy, was working with an old white journeyman by the name of Louie "Cigar" Schaefer.

It seemed like Louie, who was well into his sixties, was always smoking a cigar and constantly complaining about one foreman or another. He only had a year or so to go before he was going to retire, and he didn't like the idea of some foreman twenty or twenty-five years younger than him telling him what to do or how to do it.

Just by chance, I happened to run into Louie several years after he packed up and retired to Northeast Michigan's small but wonderful little town of Millersburg where I grew up. It was during deer season which is in the middle of November. I had just walked into the local watering hole with my cousins and there was Louie standing at the bar and talking to someone with that big old cigar sticking out of the corner of his mouth. He couldn't believe it when I came up to him. It turned out he was living on a small spread a few miles out of town where he enjoyed living in "God's Country." Unfortunately, his health failed him a few years later and he passed away.

Henry Horn and I often stopped by each other's area to talk – especially about some of the more humorous aspects of the job, and believe me, there were plenty of them.

One of the favorite tricks of some of the production workers on days when it was very hot inside of the plant, or if they just wanted a break in the action, was to toss a piece of scrap metal or even a whole part into the conveyor belt hoping that it would get hung up around the drum that turns the belt. This, in turn, would slow the line down or even stop it, which meant that the production line boss would have to contact our boss, who in turn would send a millwright over to the line to determine what needed to be done to get the line operating once again.

If the men on the line had not taken their break yet, their boss would send them on it, or if they had already been on their break, he would send them to another line. If needed, he could also break them up to go on even smaller jobs, such as a single point welder on oil pans, that only needed one worker. I was operating one of those single point welders on a particularly hot day and only had a T – shirt on with no protective apron. Well, the brass type point was starting to wear out and happened to hit slightly off center causing one huge shower of extremely hot, sparks that hit me directly in the abdomen. I'm quite sure that I must have let out a pretty good expletive when that happened. I had a big red welt there for a week or so later. Not fun! However, this usually only lasted until maintenance got the line running again and then they would round up all the workers and get them going once again.

Getting back to what originally happened, the production man could not necessarily be blamed, unless someone actually saw him sabotaging the line, because quite often, the parts on the conveyor would back up if there were problems causing a slow - down. They would then fall off of the conveyor, often ending up inside the belt, causing the same problem that they did if someone had intentionally thrown a part in there.

Something that also caused this to happen was when the scrap hoppers would back up because of some type of obstruction and the scrap parts would then start piling up. Every now and then, one would bounce into the belt causing it to stop running.

Occasionally, the production boss could get the part out without having to call maintenance, but most of the time we had to shut the line down and make some adjustments. Generally, this involved turning the "take- ups" in with a crescent wrench. This would then draw the drum in and loosen the belt enough for us to get the part out.

A lot of these parts had extremely sharp edges that would often cut the belt, so we would then have to shut the line down for an hour or so and splice a new piece of belt onto the old one, or just completely change the whole belt, which would then drive the production bosses crazy.

Speaking of crazy, some of these bosses acted like absolute idiots whenever there was a breakdown – even if it was just for just a routine breakdown.

If there was a major breakdown, all hell could break loose and often did. There would be foremen, general foreman, superintendents and managers from both production and skilled trades, and all of them would start waving their arms around and yelling and screaming. It was totally hilarious.

I once saw two superintendents, one from production, and one from maintenance, going at it nose - to – nose, screaming obscenities at each other with their faces turning beet red and ready to explode. The following day, you could see them walking down the aisle together acting as though nothing like that ever took place. Amazing, yet it wasn't uncommon for confrontations like that to take place.

If someone was caught throwing parts into a belt or otherwise messing it up, they could get three days off from work, and if it was a second or third offense, they could get a week or two off or even get fired.

With all the power that unions have – or at least had in those days – it was rather difficult to get fired. A worker would have to totally screw up big time to have that happen.

Henry also stayed in the Stamping Plant into the 80's before transferring to Rouge Steel, where he eventually ended up working for the union.

Later on, in our career's, we worked together in the Electric Arc Furnace, where he nearly got killed, but was fortunate enough to walk away with only some bruises and a couple cracked ribs.

I ended up working the midnight shift for approximately eight or nine months. I was then placed on afternoons where I worked in another production area, which was located upstairs around all of those huge, loud, presses.

This was a fairly typical set-up for most apprentices. We had to do a lot of production maintenance before we could get a better job, such as, working in a construction pool or fabrication shop.

My only previous work experience on that second floor was when I was a material handler, and I only did that a few times, so it was a whole new ballgame up there around all of those noisy presses.

In 1989, before transferring to Rouge Steel, I happened to show this poem to one of our area maintenance bosses. He liked it quite a bit and asked me if he could use it for his monthly calendar that he had distributed throughout the plant. I gave him permission to do so and I thought that it would be a good introduction to the beginning of my apprenticeship while working on the second floor in the DSP.

Another Fender

Bang, bang another fender
has been punched out.
Bang, bang the foreman is
beginning to shout.
Speed it up men, can't you
go any faster?
Sure boss, if you're looking
for a Monday afternoon disaster.
We're working at a good pace,
why should we start to race?
Everyone's rolling along pretty smooth,
let's keep it at that,
And the parts will continue to move.
Bang, bang another fender
has been punched out.
Bang, bang we knew there
was no need to shout.

I was fortunate to be paired up with an experienced journeyman millwright by the name of Pat, who taught me a lot about working on the loaders that load blank pieces of sheet metal into the giant presses. We were responsible for setting the loaders in place and adjusting them until the blanks dropped smoothly into the press.

I was already familiar with all of the conveyor work, so that was no problem, but it took a little longer to learn all of the fine tuning and other adjustments on the loader. However, after a few weeks, I was doing ok.

One of the welders that I worked with while in this second-floor area was a pleasant, rosy-cheeked, slim fellow by the name of Leo. Leo was probably in his mid to late sixties and had just started working for Ford a year or so before I met him. During the short time that I knew him, he had a big influence on my health. He ended up retiring a few years later, but not before spreading the word about healthy living to anyone who would take the time to listen to him as I did.

When Leo was younger, he had abused his body with bad eating habits, drinking and smoking too much, and as a result, he had a lot of health problems. Rather than let this get him down, he made changes to his lifestyle.

He started reading everything he could about good nutrition and healthy living. He also started taking vitamins and drinking herbal teas and using lecithin granules to help lower his cholesterol level. This, of course, was way before today's miracle–type drugs that can be taken for just about anything, but can have severe side effects.

Leo was way ahead of everyone in his healthy living theories, and I feel like I am living proof of that, because a couple years after getting married in 1975, I started to regularly find blood in my stool. My family doctor sent me to see a specialist who told me that if I did not change my diet and start eating more fruit and vegetables, I would probably end up developing colon cancer and would be more susceptible to other forms of cancer as well.

So then, instead of eating the typical processed meat sandwiches with all the salt, sugar, and preservatives in it, I packed foods such as: apples, oranges, banana's, nuts, carrots, celery, and salads with tuna or sardines.

My buddies were always kidding me about eating rabbit food, but they knew what I had been through and were always giving me encouragement and saying what a good job I was doing and wondered if it really worked.

All I can say is that after making the eating and lifestyle changes recommended by Leo and the doctor, I have not once in the past thirty-seven years had more than an occasional small drop of blood and that was from only being stressed out. That truly is amazing!

A buddy of mine used to work in another area of the second floor. In his younger days he used to drink quite a bit and he and his partner would keep a bottle of schnapps hidden in their toolbox and, occasionally, would go in there for a sip. Consequently, towards the second half of the shift, they would be feeling pretty good and quite often, if things were a little slow, they would entertain themselves by playing practical jokes on their boss, who was a rather nervous and jittery type of guy.

He was known to keep candy bars and other snacks hidden in the drawer of his desk, and these two guys knew this, so one day they found a dead mouse somewhere on the floor and hid it in his drawer next to his snacks. They had a fairly good idea when he would be coming back to his desk this particular afternoon, so they waited just out of sight.

When they finally saw him walking down the aisle in the direction of his desk, they hid out behind a large press where they could see everything. They anxiously watched as he took care of some paper work first and then opened that drawer up. I guess from what those guys said, he must have jumped a good foot in the air. They couldn't tell for sure because they were too busy laughing their guts out.

My buddy ended up going through a rough divorce, possibly caused by his drinking, but he re-married with a woman a few years later who helped him find religion, give up drinking alcohol and turn his life around. I guess it's a good thing that women can have an affect like that on men. He eventually went on to become an excellent, very proud and dedicated millwright after transferring to the steel division.

On the weekends when production wasn't running, everyone worked in the maintenance pool. We would meet in a certain area of the plant, which was usually the main lunchroom on the first floor, where the foreman would then hand out the job assignments.

Most of the time, he would match up two millwrights and a welder for each job. Sometimes, however, on bigger jobs, there would be four or five millwrights and a couple welders.

The General Foreman over the millwrights on days was a tall, medium built guy, by the name of Doug Ronan, who was one of the most knowledge-able maintenance bosses I have ever had. Each time that I had an opportunity to talk with him, I would bring up the subject of me getting out of the area and working either in the construction pool or the automation shop.

When an opening for a millwright apprentice finally came up in the automation shop, he called me aside and said something like, "You've worked in the area long enough, why don't you report to the automation shop next week."

Needless to say, I was so elated I could barely talk, but I do remember thanking him for remembering that I wanted to work there, and I told him that I really appreciated him giving me that opportunity.

However, before going on about the automation shop, I want to say a few words about a young electrician by the name of Bob King, who was working in the DSP around this time (the mid – to late – 1970's.) I remember talking with Bob a few times about some of the things that were taking place in the Rouge area and being impressed by his thoughts about various work-related problems. A couple of higher seniority millwrights and I were talking about him one day and they happened to mention how smart he was and that he was in the process of working on his law degree. A year or so later, Bob was elected president of our maintenance and construction unit. He eventually followed that up by becoming president of our local 600, which at that time was one of the biggest locals in the country, if not the biggest.

This was also only a brief stint for Bob, because he was on a fast train to succeed that eventually took him to a position where he was third in line to be president of our National UAW. Finally, in June of 2010, he was elected president of the National UAW. This was definitely no big surprise to anyone who knew him and I am proud to say that I once worked with him.

He came in during an extremely difficult time when membership was slipping and in a steep decline. All in all, he did an excellent job, even though he unfortunately, was unable to unionize some of the plants in the southern states. This was definitely a tough pill for him to swallow.

This picture of Bob King and myself was taken outside of St. Paul's Catholic church in Onaway where I am an usher and front door greeter.

I recognized him immediately as he walked up to the church and offered up a hand shake as I greeted him by his first name. I quickly introduced myself as a fellow retired skilled tradesman in the DSP while he was an electrician there and that I had just finished completing a book about the Rouge called, "Uncle Henry's Ford Rouge." He congratulated me on doing this and said he would catch up with me after Mass was over.

We ended up having a nice conversation and then I went over to my truck and signed a book for him. A few months after that he showed up again and this time, I didn't forget to ask him about having our picture taken in front of my truck.

CHAPTER 9

Bernie and the Boys in the G – Hole.

The automation shop was located across the road from the main part of the Stamping Plant. One of the ways to get to it was to walk across the road that went through a tunnel that took traffic from the east side of the complex to the west side. On the north side of the tunnel was the Stamping Plant, and on the south side was the Rolling Mill. One of the reasons why the automation shop was called the G – hole was because that was an old section of the Rolling Mill that they gave to the Stamping Plant to use for their shop.

The other way to get to this shop from inside the Stamping Plant was by walking up to the second floor and going south, over the tunnel, to where there was a balcony that overlooked the shop. At each end of the balcony was a stairway that would lead you back down to the automation shop.

The reason I mention this is because the sixty - year old plant engineering manager, B. Nunn, along with one of his top superintendents would walk throughout the plant at the beginning of the day shift.

Whenever Nunn, a very gray-haired mustached man around 5 feet – 9 inches tall, saw something he did not like, he would point it out and the superintendent would jot it down. When they would get to the south end of the building, they would look down over the balcony onto our shop, and if he saw someone who wasn't looking busy, or if the shop was looking even the slightest bit messy, we would hear about it – probably within minutes.

This was one of the main reasons there was so much tension early in the morning in our shop. Our boss, Bernie, didn't want to be getting any backlash coming down from Nunn. Therefore, he stressed that we should not get caught standing around BS-ing, or looking like we didn't have anything to do. He wanted us to at least look like we were working, even if we had to fake it, which we often kidded about doing.

By late morning and afternoon, everything was fine, but the first thing in the morning, we were like a bunch of ducks in a pond, and Nunn and his superintendent were the hunters upstairs taking shots at us. It was nothing short of brutal, because Nunn could be a real asshole and make things quite miserable for everyone, especially our boss, who just dreaded seeing him looking over that balcony.

This was one of the reasons a lot of guys preferred to work in the millwright pool, rather than in this shop. They didn't want to have to deal with Nunn.

However, even in the millwright pool, they weren't exactly exempt from Nunn's "my way or the highway" demands. More than once, workers would spend hours hanging iron for some project, and if it wasn't done close enough to the way he thought it should be done, even though it would have been better than his way, he would have the next shift tear it down and start over. This used to drive the foremen crazy. They would often tell their guys who put it up, "Hey! You did a great job and it would have worked fine, Nunn, however, wants it done his way so that's the way it's got to be.

Eventually, the union and the company established an Employee Involvement, "E. I." program. This consisted of representatives from the company, union, and the skilled trades. There were usually meetings to discuss upcoming projects, and various problems that might occur. Nunn didn't want to have anything to do with this program, but he had no choice.

We knew that it really killed him to have to do this because he could no longer bully people around the way he used to.

Our foreman over the automation shop was a medium built, dark haired guy by the name of Bernie, who was an electrician by trade. Bernie ran a very efficient shop that had a reputation for getting even the toughest projects done on or ahead of schedule. He was also quite talented when it came to solving automation problems, which would eventually become our main line of work in the automation shop. This shift towards doing more automation work, actually changed the whole atmosphere of the shop and was one of the reasons why after five years of working there, I decided to pack it in and transfer to the construction pool to work for a boss by the name of Guerro. Guerro was anxious to have me work for him because my buddy Rosey was his right-hand man at the time and told him that I would do a good job for him. I will talk about all of this later because Guerro went on to become involved in a big scandal and eventually was demoted from being a maintenance boss to being a boss over production.

At first, my main concern while working in the G – hole was to familiarize myself with my new surroundings and workers and make sure I didn't screw anything up. I just tried to work hard and show my boss, Bernie, that I would fit in really well with his crew. Speaking of the crew, I quickly learned that there were some practical jokers that I had to watch out for.

One day, I was working with this stocky, millwright leader by the name of Romanowski, who sometime later on in his career became a committeeman. We had been working on a conveyor that had been sent to our shop for repairs when he comes up to me with a Styrofoam cup and said, "Take this over to the cleaning tank and get us a small amount of that solution so we can clean the reducer up before taking it apart."

That seemed like a fairly reasonable request so I did as he said, and before I could get halfway back to the conveyor, the fluid had eaten through the Styrofoam and started leaking all over the floor. Romanowski and another millwright, Fred Goroni, who later became a good friend of mine, were standing by the conveyor laughing their butts off. I was a little embarrassed for letting myself get caught up in that situation, but I chalked it up as a lesson learned.

Another practical joker was one of our excellent welders, Ron Bycraft, who would occasionally take a water bottle fire extinguisher and squirt it high in the air near where someone was working, and then kind of nonchalantly turn away, acting like he didn't know what was happening.

Quite often if things got really slow, the guys would have an all-out water fight with the extinguishers, which, by the way, were easy to refill and re-pressurize. Fortunately, we were usually too busy for this kind of entertainment, but it was fun every once and awhile.

So, as well as learning a lot of good things working in the G – hole, there was usually something exciting going on to help keep things from becoming boring.

Most of our work in the G – hole consisted of building or repairing conveyors, automation aid for the production workers, such as stands or trays for them to put their stock in, scrap chutes, and just about anything else that production on the second floor needed. This was where all of the huge presses were located, and that was pretty much what we catered to.

Occasionally, Bernie would bring a big print down to the shop and we would then have to take it down into the little cafeteria that we had behind our shop and set it up on a long table so that we could easily study it for a period of time to figure out just what was there and what we needed to do in order to fabricate that particular project.

Bernie might have to order special lengths of certain types of steel or iron that we did not normally carry in our steel crib, and this meant that we had to wait for the material to come in before we could get started on that particular job. Even so, Bernie still had to give the department that made the request for this item to be built, a rough idea as to how long it would take to build it.

Another one of our millwright leaders, Danny, and one of our welders, usually Bycraft because he was excellent at estimating the hours it would take to weld these projects, would sit down with Bernie and figure everything out.

One of the reasons that I wanted to work in the automation shop was to get this kind of experience, so I always looked forward to working on these interesting projects and doing a good job on them.

A few months after I started working in the G – hole, I was up for my final review before graduating. Bernie liked my work and wanted to make sure he kept me in his shop, so he gave me a good grade of 100 percent.

Several weeks later, I graduated to journeyman status and ended up working in that shop for five years, some of which were quite interesting.

One year right after our Christmas break, I was standing at a large grinding wheel, grinding burrs off of some small pieces of angle iron I was working on. This little Italian welder by the name of Al Sindici, who was nicknamed "The Ghost" because of how fast he could disappear whenever we needed him to do some welding or burning, came up to me and started talking about our Christmas vacation.

I ended up getting so involved in our conversation that I lost my concentration and focus and ended up cutting my left index finger so bad that I had to go to the Central Medical building where they sewed it back up with six stitches.

"The Ghost" felt pretty bad about it because he knew he was over there distracting me. He was still apologizing weeks later. Actually, it was another good lesson learned. You should never let yourself become distracted like that when working with any kind of power tools or grinders. I should have stopped what I was doing while talking to him, finish the conversation and then return to the grinding wheel.

Another lesson learned the hard way came one day when I was sent over to the old machine shop, which was also a part of the G- hole, to help out my millwright buddy Fred Goroni. Fred was in the process of taking down a chain air hoist that was mounted on some overhead monorail.

Fred was told that the millwright pool had begun dismantling some of the frame work around the shop over the weekend, but what he didn't know was that they had burned part of the welds that were holding the framework against the side of the overhang. They had not told anyone that they had done this. As a result, all that was holding the framework up were two legs on one end and a few half - burned welds at the other end. That's all that was holding the large angle iron clips that were supporting the monorail. (Clips were used as hangers to connect something to the building framework because we could not weld anything to beams that supported the building construction, since the heat from the welds would break down the molecules in the steel, thus weakening it.)

Anyhow, what it came down to was that Fred, who was a big guy, around 6' 2" and 210 pounds and an experienced journeyman, assumed (which is usually a mistake in maintenance) that the main framework was still fastened down as it should be. Consequently, when I went over there to help him and this old electrician known as "Sailor John" pull the hoist off of the end of the monorail, the whole framework and overhead bridge that supported the monorail came down over our heads and fell on the floor and on a couple of large work tables. Fred was knocked down to the floor pretty hard, and Sailor John's shoulder was lightly grazed, but otherwise he was ok. I was extremely fortunate that all of that mess fell down without even touching me. Amazing!

The crash of all that metal made so much noise when it happened that everyone in the shop area came running over to see what happened. Our Boss, Bernie, decided that Fred needed medical attention, so a hospital van took him to the Henry Ford Hospital, where they thoroughly checked him out and finally determined that he was well enough to return to work the next day. If it wasn't for the work tables, the whole bridge would have fallen on top of us. Needless to say, we were all in shock, wondering how such a dangerous thing could have happened.

I know that there was an investigation into this accident, but I do not remember too many of the details. Someone from the millwright pool might have been written up for not welding some pieces of iron to hold the framework up, but I don't know.

Nevertheless, it was another lesson learned, and one that I never forgot. From that point on, I always double checked the other shift's work before putting myself, or anyone working with me, in a potentially dangerous situation.

The electrician, Sailor John, who was helping Fred on his job, was quite a character and reminded me a lot of the old roofer, Nick the Greek, who had such a wonderful voice. I didn't know too much about John, except that he was about 5' 10", 230 pounds, and was, shall I put it nicely, rather slow in the mental department – especially for an electrician.

The bosses usually only gave him simple electrical jobs, like repairing the hand buttons used to operate the presses. He had his own little bench area where he could strip these control units down and replace them with new wire, test them out and then stack them up ready to go back out on the floor again. We had come to the conclusion that the company was just keeping him on because of something that might have happened to him years before.

Quite often, Sailor John would sit in his chair in a corner of the shop during his break or at lunchtime and fall asleep with his mouth wide open and flies buzzing all around him. He sincerely was a nasty smelling man. We would just shake our head and say something about writing a book sometime about all of the weird characters we knew at Ford.

Another welder in the G – hole was a tall, black guy named J.C., who helped me learn a lot of tricks about welding when doing fabricating work. Light tack welds just enough to hold the part together were important. That way everything could be double checked to make sure it was all squared up before the rest of the welding took place.

Welders didn't like to have to burn something apart and then have to re-weld it, so the millwrights had to make sure that they got everything right the first time. This was much easier to do in a shop than when we were out on a tough job somewhere inside the plant with a breakdown that needed to be a rush job.

One year at a Christmas party, J. C. brought in a loaf of zucchini bread that his wife had made. It had pineapple, raisins, and walnuts, along with the zucchini in it and was excellent. I liked it so much he brought in the recipe for me and today my wife, Debbie, still makes it.

I noticed that our boss, definitely had a problem with certain black millwrights who would sometimes be sent down to the shop to do some work for us when we got back-logged. He just didn't trust them to do a good job. He thought that they did not care enough about the quality of work that they put out and therefore, he was always trying to find some reason to keep them out of his shop.

Here's an example; One day the boss over the millwright pool sent two guys down to the automation shop to help repair a conveyor. The one guy was a big, tall friendly fellow by the name of Mel, who I knew from my production days, and the other guy was a slim fellow called Dave, and who was better known as Super Fly because of the sharp way he dressed when not in his work cloths.

Neither one of these guys were dummies. In fact, I think that's what bothered our boss. He felt that they were always scheming of ways to screw him. As it turned out, something happened with their job that caused him to write them up. I think that they might have accidently dropped the bottom frame of the conveyor from the crane, which caused it to get twisted and made for a lot more work.

It was just an inadvertent accident that could have happened to anyone, but he didn't particularly care for these guys, so he used this as an excuse to get them. If it had been anyone else, he would have been upset, but there's no way that he would have written them up.

Obviously, they weren't too happy about this, so they made a big squawk about it. They told their committeeman what happened and also said that if he was going to write them up for what they did, he should also write up Ralph Bowman and me for a minor problem we had caused the day before when we accidentally bent up a small part of a drive unit on the end of a conveyor.

Ralph Bowman was a big white guy who had been working in the shop for about a year or so and was a good worker, but sometimes things just happen no matter how careful you are.

And, that's exactly what happened on this particular day. Ralph was lowering the conveyor with the radio-controlled crane box and I was steadying the sides of it. As he set it down, the end of the drive unit bumped a little too hard against the table causing a small amount of damage. It wasn't any big deal and was something that we were able to repair quite easily. However, these two guys saw us mess up and so they demanded that our boss write us up also – even though the damage to the conveyor frame that they had caused was much more extensive than ours.

So now our boss had dug a hole for himself and was trying to get out of it, and he wanted my partner and me to help bail him out by "letting" him write us up. He told us he would take it off of our record after sixty days or whenever the expiration date was up for the report. Bowman and I weren't too happy about this, but we let him go ahead and do it. From that day on however, our boss lost a lot of credibility in my mind, which factored in quite heavily when I left the automation shop about a year or so later.

One day while taking our break in the G – hole lunchroom, Fred Goroni and I were sitting at a table BS-ing when all of a sudden, we heard a loud noise that had come from a huge explosion in an electrical substation that supplied electricity to the south end of the Stamping Plant.

The substation was just outside of the cafeteria and the explosion caused the walls to tremble. Everyone in the lunchroom immediately jumped up and ran out to see just exactly what happened.

There was hot, poisonous smoke coming out of the substation that filled half of the Stamping Plant, and which caused management to shut it down for the rest of the day. Obviously, they didn't want poisonous chemicals such as PCBs leaking from the station and filtering throughout the plant.

I'm quite sure that everyone in the lunchroom will never forget that day and probably gives thanks that it was not any worse than what it was. We could easily have been injured or even killed if one of the walls had been blown out.

We were also fortunate that no one was walking past the station when the explosion occurred, because if they were, they probably would not be around today to tell about it. Amazing!

Fred and I often worked together, so I have another story to tell about a job that we were assigned late one afternoon after the end of our day shift. I cannot remember for sure, but evidently, we were working four hours over.

We had to go upstairs on the balcony over the shop and hook up a large automated loader and then let the overhead crane operator set it down on a large flatbed truck trailer that was waiting below.

The driver of this sharp–looking, brand new, Kenworth truck was a young kid who was really proud of his shiny new paint job with detailed writing glistening in the sunshine. Fred and I were down there talking with him and you could tell he really loved that truck.

Unfortunately for this kid, the crane operator was an old guy who had some past disciplinary problems for carelessness. As he was bringing the automated loader over the truck, he started to lower it a little too fast and lost control, causing it to swing into the rear of the awesome looking Kenworth trucks cab. This quite obviously caused some extensive damage to this young guy's truck that he was so proud of. I think I saw the kid's eyes welling up with tears after he finally got a grip on what had happened. I know he probably felt like climbing up into the cab of that crane and choking that old boy to death.

That, however, wasn't the only damage the old coot did. The expensive piece of automation he was lowering had some parts knocked off of it, which would have to be replaced before it could leave the shop, so now the cost of the damage was even more and the project would have to be delayed.

Needless to say, that was the operator's last stand. The union could not cover for him anymore, and so the company forced him into retiring effective immediately. Ford would end up having to pay to have the kid's truck repaired, and it also lost money by having to repair the loader. So, there was only one way out for the crane operator, and that was a trip down the highway.

Whenever there was a nasty storm outside, we would often walk over to the large truck doors that were usually open and check out the severity of the weather. On this one particular day, a really bad storm with high winds came up rather quickly. The sky turned a deep, dark green color and the rain was pouring down in sheets. Fred and I strolled over to see what was going on outside, when all of a sudden, as we looked across the Rouge River to where a large iron ore ship was being unloaded by an overhead crane operator, a huge wind swept through and took the operator and the long extension boom that his cab was attached to and swept them both into the river.

Fred and I just looked at each other in disbelief, shaking our heads and saying something like, "Holy shit, did you see that?" The poor crane operator went right into the drink. We ended up finding out the next day that although the operator was quite shaken up, he was pulled safely from the river and was ok. He had been able to stay with the extension until help was able to rescue him. The official weather report said that a small tornado had ripped through that area around the time this incident took place, which wasn't too long before our quitting time at 3:30 pm.

Speaking of the rain storm, the ground floor in the DSP was made out of concrete, but was protected by wooden blocks approximately 2 1/2" high x 4" wide and about 8" long laid on top of it. Quite often, water from hard rains or large oil spills would seep underneath these blocks, which would then absorb the liquid and cause them to swell up – sometimes as high as

15" – 20". This always made a big mess and kept the floor block men busy replacing and resetting the blocks all the time.

These floor blocks would also be susceptible to picking up small pieces of scrap steel, so in order to keep the floor clean and prevent injuries, large floor scrubbing machines were constantly making their rounds.

I happened to find out the hard way just how dangerous scrap steel sticking out of a piece of wooden floor block can be as one penetrated my tennis shoe as I was walking out of the plant one night. I had to be taken to the Central Medical building where they had to freeze the area and then cut or pull the piece out and then clean the aching wound up and bandage it. I ended up gimping around for a week or so afterward.

The second story floors had ¾" steel floor plate set over structured beams and then had either these wood floor blocks laid on top of them or, in some areas where more reinforcement was required, they used 2 ½" x 30" square blocks made out of individual pieces of pecan wood that had strong rods running through them to hold everything together.

In the meantime, there were changes going on in the Stamping Plant that had a huge effect on our automation shop. In the early 1980's, robots and automated production were growing bigger and bigger. Lines that used to have eight or eleven men were now operating with significantly fewer workers. In fact, some jobs would have fewer than half the amount of workers it took to do the same job only a year or so earlier.

Because of this influx of automated equipment, our shop was becoming overloaded with work because repairing these complicated machines was very similar to the other machine repair work we were already doing. I didn't mind it too much at first because there was so much to learn, but after so many months of doing basically the same thing over and over, I started to get tired of it and longed for more of the real millwright work.

To make matters even worse, the company had brought in a new guy by the name of Red Mead who was known as an automation expert, and made him the general foreman in charge of our automation shop.

All of the guys in the shop knew that this was really bothering our boss and eventually it led to a lot of friction between the two men. Bernie usually tried to outdo him, and Mead did his best not to let Bernie get the better of him concerning different ideas, such as how to make certain types of equipment run more efficiently.

The reason that I am mentioning this is because Mead, who was a tall, thin, light haired, balding guy with a cocky attitude, was thought to have stolen a great idea that was Bernie's. As a result, he was also thought to have won a very nice suggestion award prize. The awards could be quite gratifying. For example, a buddy of mine, Mark Plave, who I worked production with back around 1968 – 70, won a new car as an award, which at that time was worth around $6,000.

So things were changing, almost too fast, in the G – hole. Even though I still enjoyed going upstairs and watching a line run and then try to figure out how to eliminate some of the problems that they were complaining about, I was definitely getting tired of what was going on in the shop and was ready to become a member of the millwright pool on days.

Also, about this same time, I started to carpool with a fellow millwright and neighbor, Jimmy "Rosey" Rosenau, who lived on the cross street behind our house in Livonia.

Rosey, who was several years younger than me stood around 5' 7" and weighed about 155 – 160 pounds, was a very friendly person, but not someone you would want to double–cross.

On this one particular occasion, a millwright by the name of Rodriguez, who was just slightly taller and heavier than Rosey, found out the hard way that he wasn't someone to mess with. Rosey and Rodriguez were working as partners in a production area upstairs and it seemed that every-time there was a breakdown, Rodriguez would mysteriously disappear until Rosey had completed most of or all of the work and then finally reappearing. Finally, after this went on too many times, Rosey got fed up with this guy's little game and took him off to the side of a press and just about choked him to death while threatening to hang him up from a hook that was welded on the side of the press. Needless to say, he didn't have any more problems with the guy.

Without a doubt, Rosey was one of the best and hardest working mill-wrights I have ever known. While car-pooling, we used to discuss all of our day's problems on the drive home every afternoon, and he finally talked me into leaving the automation shop and working with him in the millwright pool for a short, medium built guy by the name of Guerro.

I had not informed Bernie yet of my plans to leave, but word filtered down to him and so he asked me if it was true. I said, "Yes, I've been here in the G – hole for five years and I am ready for a change. Besides that, I'm just kind of fed up with the way things have been going lately, and so therefore, I'm ready to move on." Well, he wasn't too happy about my decision and tried to persuade me to stay, but my mind was made up, and there was to be no turning back.

"Red" Mead, the general foreman over the shop, even tried to convince me to stay. I just told him the same thing that I had said to Bernie. I was ready to move on, and no-one was going to change my mind. And, my pay scale was already set and so there was no way I could get a raise unless I was made a leader and the shop already had enough leaders, who were paid 50 cents an hour more than a regular millwright. I probably still would not have stayed anyhow, so it really didn't matter.

About the only thing I knew about Guerro at this time came from working for him occasionally on a weekend. He seemed to come across as a hot – shot, unscrupulous type of guy, and now that I was working for him every day, I could see some of the questionable things he was doing.

A good example was this one quiet Sunday when Guerro assigned Rosey, who was one of his millwright leaders, me, and a welder to do a job. We could not have been on the job for more than a half hour when Guerro came over to me and said, "I need to take Rosey on another job for a while, so you and Jackson can handle this job until he gets back." Well, we didn't see Rosey for the rest of the day because Guerro knew that he was a good automobile mechanic and so he had him working on his car at the north end of the building close to where there was a parking spot for bosses. This area of the building was on the main floor where the scrap system was located, and on weekends, it was usually pretty quiet around there because nothing much was running and therefore there was no one around. It was a good time and place to do a "government job", which was a personal job that didn't pertain to work.

This was the type of guy we were dealing with and most of the millwrights who had been working for him for a while knew it. Therefore, we were not too real surprised when he became the central person under investigation when some toolboxes were broken into and both personal and company tools came up missing.

It happened on one particular Easter weekend when a bunch of toolboxes were broken into. I was fortunate that the thief or thieves stopped just before they got to the area where mine was located. Other tool boxes had been hit earlier, shortly after the first of the year, probably while we were still on Christmas vacation.

Quite often, outside contractors were responsible for these thefts, but this time, it appeared that this was not the case. It had all the markings of an inside job.

The reason I mention this is because a young millwright by the name of Danny told some guys that Guerro was talking to him one day while he was standing next to Danny's open tool box, and that Guerro seemed to take an extraordinary interest in some of his personal tools that were in the box.

This was maybe two or three weeks before someone broke into Danny's toolbox on a quiet Sunday by using a burning torch to burn his lock off. The thief then took a good number of his tools, some of which were quite expensive. To say the least, Danny was very upset. The company had plant security and maintenance supervision check everything out and file reports. Company tools would be replaced, but not the expensive personal tools and that's what got Danny's dander up.

Remembering how interested Guerro was a few weeks earlier while standing near his tool box, Danny's natural reaction was to suspect Guerro of committing the crime. However, he had no proof, so he set out to do some investigating.

One day while Guerro was at work, Danny, who knew where Guerro lived drove by his house and parked his car on the side of the street. He then went up to his house pretending that he had a flat tire and asked his wife if he could borrow a wrench. She did exactly what Danny was hoping she would do and that was open the garage door where Danny's tools were clearly in sight and easy to see.

I'm not sure of what exactly happened next. I think Danny made the mistake of leaving without calling the cops, or at least get some witnesses over there. Guerro's wife became suspicious and called him at work. He came home as soon as he could and got rid of all the tools. When Danny came back sometime later with a witness and or the authorities, there were no tools to be found that belonged to him. They were all gone – as though that was a big surprise.

Today where nearly everyone has a cell phone that can take great pictures there would not have been any problems. He would have had Guerro by the balls.

As a result of all of this, Guerro was never prosecuted for the theft, but he did receive some time off from work and then was transferred out of the plant into another building in the Rouge, only to return a year or so later. When he returned, I was one of a group of millwrights and welders who refused to work for him. We had the union force the company into taking him off of maintenance and making him a production boss.

I can still remember us talking about this when there were rumors that he might be coming back to our shift to work. The most commonly asked question was, "Would you work for him?"

I guess we couldn't understand how or why the company would let him come back, because everyone knew that there was no question that he was a thief, and therefore, we were all quite upset about having to possibly work for him.

So, the day finally arrived when he came around with the lineup. Guess who he came up to first? You got it. Mister Softy, he must have thought, but no way Jose! I refused to take the job assignment from him. Rosey had been promoted to a foreman's position, so he wasn't around to help bail him out – not that he would have anyway after what happened.

Guerro kind of shook his head and went on to someone else, but it wasn't going to work. Every last one of us refused to work for him. He ended up having to call the general foreman, who quickly figured out what was going on. He took the assignment sheet and lined us all up with jobs, and sent us on our way, saying he would call our committeeman over to try and settle the matter, because we told him that we absolutely would not work for this man.

After meeting with the union people, a decision was made to let Guerro work as a production foreman. Most of us felt that he was very fortunate to even be able to get this job. I don't believe I ever spoke with him again, and I was glad that I stood up to him and set an example for the rest of the men.

The man who eventually took Guerro's place was a short, stocky guy by the name of Zaya, who had been working as a maintenance boss upstairs around the production lines.

As the boss over the pool, Zaya soon developed a reputation for doing all kinds of crazy things. Most of the higher seniority millwrights thought of him as some sort of idiot because of all the goofy things he wanted them to do. It was absolutely ridiculous!

Before Employee Involvement was established, he used to have his millwrights do whatever it took to get his jobs done, even if that meant "stealing" a lift or cherry picker (portable crane) from another trade's job.

For instance, another crew of skilled tradesmen, let's say the pipefitters, were using a lift to hang some pipe for a job that they had been doing for several days. One of Zaya's crews might be on a hot job that needed a lift, but the problem was that there were no lifts available. They were all being used. So Zaya would hop on his little electric scooter cart and drive around the plant until he comes upon the one that the pipefitters are using. No one is around, so Zaya, instead of contacting their boss or the crew's leader on that job to ask if his crew could borrow the lift for a while, goes back to his men and tells them to hurry up and go get the lift and use it on their job.

This almost always caused a big problem, and after a few bad experiences, we started to question Zaya's judgement and tried to work things out a bit more diplomatically with whoever was using the equipment we needed.

After Employee Involvement was established, Zaya and some of the other bosses who I have already mentioned, had to make more of an effort to get along with everyone and refrain from all the crazy things they had been used to doing in the past.

Shortly after the Guerro fiasco, things started to look pretty bleak in the DSP, as well as in the other plants. Layoffs were being announced, and there was talk about permanently closing some of the plants – specifically the Stamping and Assembly Plants.

CHAPTER 10

Guaranteed Employment Numbers

The work force in the DSP was cut back drastically, and I ended up having no choice but to bump a young guy from the Glass Plant, which came back to haunt me, because he made his decision to be placed into the Guaranteed Employment Numbers (GEN) program, which would let workers who were laid off take a job in a plant outside of the Rouge if there was an opening.

I did not want to go into this GEN program because once you were in it, you had to take whatever job came up anywhere in the country, or you risked going to the bottom of the list. And, if you were in the program, you were restricted as to how many hours you could work.

So not wanting to take a chance and end up somewhere in Ohio or Kentucky, I decided to stay in the Rouge system and roll the dice.

Anyhow, this young millwright that I bumped ended up getting a job at the Wayne Trucking Plant, which was only fifteen miles from my house. Compare that to the thirty miles I ended up having to drive once my family and I moved into our new house just outside of Plymouth. Of course, he had to come around and brag about getting so lucky. I obviously wasn't too happy about it, but there was nothing I could do or say that would make a difference. That's just the way the ball bounces sometimes.

Another time that I missed out on a good job was when another buddy of mine, Paul Stanley, who also signed up for the GEN program, took a job at the Milan Plastic Plant. Which was a really nice, relatively clean, and quiet factory to work in.

While still in the Stamping Plant, Stanley and I teamed up to form what the afternoon boss, Glenn T. McGrew, called "The A – Team." He called us this because we were always called in to do the hot jobs that had to have a lot of work done in a short amount of time. We would go in and get a new job set up and going real well before his afternoon shift came in and took over. The bosses liked this because it made everything that much easier for their guys to come in and follow up on what we were doing.

A couple of years later, the Milan Plastic Plant needed some additional help on the weekends because they were behind on some big project. I had the opportunity to go out there and work for about a month or so on Saturdays and Sundays because work was still rather slow in the DSP. It turned out to be a very nice place to work, and I would have loved to worked there permanently, I however, had to go back to the DSP on Mondays, which was always tough and just made me more upset about missing out on these jobs.

One time before coming back to the DSP, I was working afternoons in the Glass Plant for a foreman by the name of Billy Baltimore. Baltimore was a good boss who had some past disciplinary problems for alcohol consumption. I liked him quite a bit because he was smart and very knowledgeable about the jobs, and he had a good sense of humor. Besides that, he wasn't afraid to back his men up if there were any problems. And of course, we all appreciated that.

One excruciatingly hot, Sunday afternoon in the middle of the summer, I was assigned a job changing bearings on some circulating fans that were located on top of a heating station in a rather confined area. There was very little air flow up there, and as you can imagine, it was extremely hot. My partner, whose name was Tim, was a tall, medium built white guy, who I had known since the days when he first started working in the DSP, which was probably a couple of years before this. Tim and I had a few things in common, such as sports, and in particular all of the major Detroit sports teams. Also, there was the fact that we lived not too far from each other. Sometime after lunch towards the end of our last break, Baltimore came around to check on us. He could easily see that we were soaking wet and not exactly having a lot of fun up there in all that heat. He asked us how we were doing and if there was anything he could get for us. We told him we were having some trouble getting some of the bearings off, and that we would need some more spray cans of penetrating oil to facilitate the loosening of these burned up old bearings. Before he left to get the oil, I jokingly said, "Yeah, and we could use a couple of cold Buds also." He just kind of grinned as he left and we went back to work not thinking any thing of it. About twenty minutes or so later, he came back with what looked like our spray oil, but surprise, it was four cans of Budweiser beer.

Tim and I just looked at each other and smiled. Billy handed the piwa, beer in Polish, to us and just said to be careful. It's getting near the end of the shift, and I appreciate you guys doing a good job up there in all that heat. Then he proceeded to hand us up some more spray oil and as he did, we thanked him for the brewskis. After he disappeared, we just shook our heads and said, "Man, I can't believe he did that." We sat up there and drank our refreshing beer and then finished our last bearing and then cleaned the place up. It was an experience that I will never forget.

Another night in the Glass Plant that I will never forget was the time I was assigned to work at the north end of the building as a stand-by in case the furnace workers, who were changing heating elements in this one furnace, needed any help. It was a special job that they did only every so often, and on this particular night, they had to call this special trouble shooter guy to come in because they were having too many problems trying to accomplish their mission. He really knew what he was doing when it came to these types of situations and was more or less used to being called in at all different times for jobs such as this.

He was a red-faced, Scottish guy, about 5'-10" and around 170 lbs. and had to squeeze his, beyond middle aged butt, into some sort of asbestos, heat shield suit, to protect himself from the intense heat of the furnace.

After he completed his task, which only seemed to take a few minutes, but probably was longer, he came out with a much redder face than, I would think was normal, and then stepped outside for a while to cool off. I was told that he had always done this in the past even if it was freezing outside, which was just the case this particular evening.

After a short time, he came back in and sat down on one of the electric, scooter carts that the foremen used to run around the plant. About a minute or so later, he just keeled over and fell to the floor.

Our millwright foreman who was standing nearby, reacted immediately, and quickly ran over to help him. He could easily see that the guy wasn't breathing, so he started administering CPR. In the meantime, someone called the plant fire department, which fortunately, was right next door to the Glass Plant, so help was there in no time. They quickly took over and hooked the guy up to oxygen, but it was to no avail. He died before they could get him to the hospital.

Our boss did a great job of trying to revive him, and was completely drained when the firefighters finally got there and took over. I'm sure it is something he has never forgotten.

To me this was, unfortunately, another example of the many dangers that were constantly lurking in our workplace. Skilled tradesmen not only in the Rouge, but everywhere, have to be keenly aware of what's going on around them at all times and be ready to react when something out of the ordinary happens. It is without a doubt why so many of the old tradesmen, in the Rouge were as grumpy as they were. They had probably been injured far too many times than they would like to admit when they were younger and did not want some young green horn screwing up and causing them to get injured just before they retire. Can't blame them. Working in a complex as huge as the Rouge and trying to do a good job without messing up your body was not always an easy thing to do, as you will find out as this story continues.

Another interesting experience in the Glass Plant was watching the production workers laminate the windshields in what was called "The White House." This was a room that was extremely cold inside and everything in it was white, even the coveralls on the workers.

Workers would take a thin sheet of plastic and lay it on one side of the windshield and then lay another side of the windshield on top of that, and then it would be set on a steel frame shaped in the size of a windshield. It would then be carried down a conveyor line where it would pass through a small furnace that would bake the plastic and glass. Eventually it would come out the other side to cool down and be stacked up ready to go out the door to an assembly line. At the time, Ford was making the Mustang in the assembly plant next door to the Glass Plant, so it's possible that a good deal of these windshields were going over there. Others were probably shipped to other plants outside of the Rouge.

After about a year of working in the Glass Plant, I was bumped out of there, by a higher seniority millwright. I ended up going back to the Stamping Plant, where things were finally starting to pick up a little, but they still weren't going at the pace they once were.

CHAPTER 11

Shift Changes in the DSP

Since there was a lack of overtime at the Stamping Plant, a lot of the higher seniority millwrights left and went over to the Steel Division, where they could get plenty of overtime and make much more money. This, of course, was always the bottom line. Many of these guys had big payments and so therefore they wanted as much overtime as they could get.

My buddy Fred Goroni had opted to leave, and so did a millwright by the name of Glen Breeding, who was perhaps the best all-around millwright in the whole Rouge Complex.

I really missed not having Glen around because I always learned so much from him. He was very sharp in all aspects of the trade, but was a rather quiet guy who didn't say too much. So, when he did say something, you had better be listening because he wouldn't put up with someone who wasn't trying to get better.

He nearly always got the biggest or most important job in the plant, and that's why I considered myself lucky anytime I was assigned to work with him.

After Glen and several other senior millwrights left, I became one of the higher seniority millwrights in the plant, and was able to hold days or even midnights, whichever shift I preferred.

So sometime around 1984 or 1985, I went on midnights for about a year. I ended up becoming partners with another Polish guy, Carl Rawski, a semi-pudgy, 5'-10" guy, who had just transferred from the Wayne Trucking Plant with a buddy of his named Big Al Hughes.

Carl and Big Al, who stood around 6'-6" and weighed nearly 270 lbs., were both on supervision at the Wayne Plant. I believe Carl was a general foreman and Al was a foreman, and due to some internal problems at the plant, they decided to leave and come to the Rouge as millwrights so they would have more opportunities to get back into supervision. Most notably, they wanted jobs somewhere in the Steel Division, which was exactly what happened about a year or so later. If you might be wondering how they were able to do all of this, it was because they were a part of our local 600. A lot of the guys weren't too happy about this, but there wasn't too much that could be done about it.

So anyhow, at that time we were working nights in the DSP and having fun. Working with a former general foreman was quite an experience because Carl knew all the tricks of the trade and he used to drive the different foremen we worked for absolutely crazy. He was always trying to out-smart them in some way or another. Usually, it was in a rather playful way, rather than to do something that would cause the boss to get all pissed off at us.

He was a good worker and together, we always kept our boss pretty happy, although maybe a little jittery at times. We would make some of the hard jobs look easy, and although Rawski liked messing with the boss, we always did our best to make sure he looked good in front of the top brass, because that was good for us too.

Our welder on midnights, was Bill "Willie" Jackson, a balding white guy about 5'-7", 170 pounds, and a few years younger than myself. Willie was quite a character and would sit on the seat on the back of our welding rig that was mounted kind of high and yell at everyone as we drove by. It was just his way of having fun, and that was cool, but too often he would get a little carried away and then we would have to yell at him to shut the hell up!

When Jackson and I had to go on days about a year or so later, he ended up taking over a welding tractor. Since he was an antique car buff who liked his vehicles to look real sharp, shiny and bright, he got a bunch of spray paint cans from the crib and painted the tractor to his satisfaction. I mean, he had this bad boy looking cool as hell. It had racing stripes and two or three different coats of paint, and God pity anyone who messed with it because Jackson had the plant engineering manager on his side.

That's right. Bob Nunn knew Jackson was real hyper, but he also knew he was a good, hard-working welder who took pride in the way his rig looked. Therefore, anyone else who used that rig had better be careful with it, because if they weren't Jackson would complain to Nunn, and then Nunn would get on the maintenance boss to make sure his men kept that tractor clean.

It seemed like every time we saw Jackson when he wasn't working, he was wiping down his welding leads and torch hose, or touching up bare spots with a can of paint that he always kept inside his rig. He was a truly amazing guy, but to his credit, he set a good example for taking care of equipment and keeping it looking good.

If you were to ask anyone in the DSP skilled trades unit in the late 1970's and early to mid-80's if there was one character that stood out during that time, they would nearly all say, "the welder Jackson."

Willie Jackson was actually a very good-hearted man, who was always willing to help out, and would do just about anything for someone else, especially if it had to do with cars.

As I said before, he was very hyper and, to put it mildly, a little different. He seemed to be a person who was starving for attention. He wasn't married, and most of us who knew him figured no woman would ever be willing to put up with someone as hyper as he was.

Jackson's whole world revolved around cars, especially cars from the late '50s up to the '70s. He owned about four old cars that he kept spotless. One was an all-black Dodge Challenger, which was his favorite. He would only take it out of the garage occasionally to show it off.

One day, he drove it over to my house in Livonia. My wife Debbie fell in love with it and wanted me to try and get him to sell it to us, but of course, there was no way that was ever going to happen.

He also owned a very sharp looking '65 Mustang and an all-white Chevy Nova that he used to drive to work when we car pooled with Rosey and another neighbor of ours, Don Pokorny, who lived only two houses from mine and whose daughters used to babysit for our girls.

After the end of our day shift this one afternoon, Rosey, Jackson, Don and myself were out in the parking lot looking all over for Jackson's Nova, and unfortunately, we couldn't find it anywhere. Someone had stolen this beautiful car of his and it made him totally sick. Who could blame him? We ended up having to call one of our wives to come and pick us up. Jackson's Nova was never found, and we had to hear about it every day for several weeks. After that experience, he bought a junker car to drive to work because he didn't want to risk losing another one of his precious collector cars.

Of course, he couldn't stand to drive the junker car the way it looked, so he had some work done on it to make it look a little better, but not so good that he had to worry about it being stolen.

While on days I also ended up working with another young millwright buddy of mine named Al Kukan. I only worked with Al for a short time, maybe six months or so, before he got bumped out of the Stamping Plant and into the Glass Plant. Those days were rough on the younger skilled tradesmen because we never knew when something like this was going to happen. It was extremely stressful to say the least.

I think the one thing I remember best about those days of working with Al was the comical things that were going on with our boss, who just happened to be Zaya, who was about to have his last hoorah in the DSP.

This time, however, it didn't have anything to do with his dealings with his fellow bosses, but with the production people.

Zaya was always in a hurry and would go flying around the plant on his little orange, electric scooter rather recklessly. One time he ran into a woman because of his carelessness, but fortunately for her, she wasn't injured too badly. However, he wasn't so lucky the next time he ran into someone.

The head cribs-man downstairs was a nice old, tall white dude by the name of Bill. We, however, called him "Hoppy" because he walked with a real obvious limp. On weekends, he often had to work in the crib upstairs and rather than use the stairway, he would walk up and down the truck ramp that connected the first and second floors because that was much easier for him. On one weekend, he was near the bottom of the ramp and unfortunately for him, Zaya came flying around the corner and wiped him out. That's right! He hit him pretty good, knocking him down and injuring his foot and leg.

I am not sure if it was the same leg that he was already limping on, but it did not matter. The point was this reckless man hurt another employee and this time they gave him thirty days off, and when he came back to work, he had to walk everywhere he went, which was a total hindrance to a maintenance boss. He eventually was transferred out of the DSP to the Wixom Assembly Plant where Lincoln's were fabricated. My Dad was one of the first millwrights hired in that plant when it first opened up in April of 1957.

Three years after the accident, I bumped into (no pun intended) Hoppy at the Henry Ford Hospital. He said he was still having problems as a result of that accident. I don't know if he received any kind of settlement out of it, but he certainly should have.

It was around the spring of 1986 when things started to look really bleak again. Rosey, who had taken a supervisory position, became tired of not getting any overtime, because of the fact that he was now at the bottom of the seniority list of foremen and also because things were just plain slow.

So, he made a decision to go back into coveralls as a millwright in the steel division, where there was an opening and where he would have a great opportunity to work all of the overtime he wanted, which of course would lead to making more greenbacks, and that essentially was what most of us wanted to do.

This meant that our car pool was now down to just Jackson, Don Pokorny and myself, and that was also to be short-lived because Don decided to transfer to steel with Jackson following a short time later.

The mid-80's was a very unstable period in the skilled trades unit at the Rouge and the millwrights were probably hit harder than any other trade, mainly because there were so many of us.

The constant talk of plant closings and layoffs had everyone on edge. (You would have to put yourself in our shoes to imagine what it was actually like. Believe me it wasn't fun!) So, because of this, there was a lot of talk going on as to how things could be made better. And most of this talk came from an average size, balding, white millwright by the name of Bennie Farrell. The first time I met Bennie I was working as an apprentice in the Rolling Mill and now here he was working as a millwright in the Stamping Plant.

Motor-mouth Bennie, as he was often called, was a very controversial guy, who it seemed was always in trouble with supervision because he was constantly complaining about something or another. I wish I could say he always had a good reason for all the chirping that he did, but I can't because Bennie Farrell did not need a good reason to complain. He would find anything to bitch about just to get on the bosses' nerves, and believe me, he did get on their nerves. They hated to see him coming because they always knew he was going to give them a headache.

One weekend, I was working with Bennie and he suggested going to Bronco's for lunch – his treat. Since he was running for committeeman, I figured he was trying to sew up another vote, but I was willing to listen to what he had to say for a free lunch.

Throughout the years that I knew Bennie, he did seem to be very committed to doing as good a job as he could possibly do as a committee-man for our local 600, which in those days was the largest in the world. His mouth, however, got him into so much trouble, it seemed he could never hold the position for any length of time.

Anyhow, our lunch at the very popular Bronco's Lounge on this particular day was a Reuben sandwich with steak fries, a beer, and an eyeful of beautiful young waitresses dressed in see-through fish net tops and Playboy bunny bottoms.

Yes, Bronco's was a small, narrow bar off of Schaffer Road and south of Michigan Avenue in Dearborn, which was a money-making bonanza for its owners. Fridays especially were extremely busy, elbow to elbow sometimes, because the workers would stop by and cash their paychecks from a little fortress-type room near the back of the bar.

As you entered into the bar there was a bar box pool table in a corner to the left where, when the place wasn't overly busy, which wasn't too often, some big money games took place. Most of the time however, it was too difficult to play because the place was always so crowded you could barely move around.

Bronco's was not only known to the many Ford Rouge employees, but it was also popular with many Ford salaried workers, such as, clay modelers and designers who worked in studios located in many of the buildings bordering the Rouge.

Truck drivers from all over the country were familiar with Bronco's also, and they used to stop by whenever they were in the area, which was usually quite often because of all the deliveries they had to make at the Rouge.

The women, of course are what made Bronco's so appealing and many of them came from all different parts of the country. Taking this job offered them a good opportunity to make a lot of money in a short period of time while learning their way around the city.

The owners also had another bar near Eagle Pass called the Mustang that was similar to Bronco's. It catered to a lot of the workers from Ford's Galvanizing Plant off of Miller Road as well as to other small businesses in the area and, of course, to the truck drivers.

Bronco's however was the biggest money maker. More than once, guys would go in there at lunchtime and never make it back to work. I've seen and heard of skilled tradesmen, designers, even some bosses, you name it, go in there for lunch and never make it out until many hours later. They would be willing to get docked the rest of the day and risk pissing off their supervisors just to stay in there and visit with the good-looking young ladies. And yes, we did make it back to work on time that day – as difficult as it was to do.

Bennie Farrell left the DSP for the Steel Division, I believe around the early '80's, and that probably wasn't soon enough as far as many of the foremen and superintendents were concerned.

I ran into him again sometime in the mid- 90's after I transferred to Rouge Steel. I believe he was back working as a committeeman.

So, once again, things were changing pretty fast in the Rouge, and as though we didn't have enough problems to deal with, there was now talk that Ford was going to close its Coke Ovens Plant. In March of 1987 Ford announced that it, indeed, was closing the plant because the company could buy coke cheaper from outside sources.

What this meant, of course, was that all of the skilled tradespeople, as well as production employees, were going to have to be absorbed by other facilities, and if they had higher seniority than someone else, they could bump that person onto a shift they might not be too happy with. This, combined with all the other negative things that were happening throughout the '80's had everyone walking around with long faces and feeling very depressed. As a result, of all of this mess, I wrote the following poem that will lead off the rather humorous story of my three-year stay on afternoons, working for the man I called the General: Glenn T. McGrew.

CHAPTER 12

The General's Boys

We are the men and women of the Rouge

We are the men and women of the Rouge.
We work hard for our bread.
Auto's assembled as fast as a Luge.
Under skies that are usually red.

We have been around for many years
and seen people come and go.
Now it looks as though we will be shedding some tears
because the Rouge will soon be the next to go.

Down through the years,
We've given her our best.
Now they say it's time to let her rest.
She's been on her last leg before,
But now it looks like this is it,
Out the door.

There are many things we can say,
But probably not enough to help her stay.
Ford has made up its mind to shut her down.
Now all we can do is walk around with a frown.
We are the men and women of the Rouge
We work hard for our bread.

Now we are trying to beat the spread,
Under odds that are very huge.
We are the men and women of the Rouge.

One of the first things McGrew said to me when I first arrived on his afternoon shift was, "You've come a long way, baby," which was in reference to when I first met him in the Engine Plant back in 1967 when I was a young, college student, cribs-man handing out coveralls and gloves and he was a young millwright just starting out.

Now, here I was working for him, not by choice however, and feeling a little rebellious because I had just lost my good day shift job and was forced to work afternoons for the first time since my production days in the DSP.

Even though I had never worked for McGrew before, I was more than familiar with his tough guy image and no-nonsense manner, which was actually a bit of a façade. He definitely liked having this type of reputation and wanted everyone to believe that he was one tough ombre. However, after working for him for several years, I found that if you gave him a fair effort, he would treat you fair in return. But, if you tried to screw him, you would be in big trouble, as many guys found out.

Glenn McGrew wasn't a real big guy, but he wasn't small either. He stood about 6' tall, and weighed maybe 180 pounds, and was a black belt martial arts expert, who taught martial arts to the Dearborn Police Department. So, you can plainly see he was no-one to fool around with.

We had another young millwright boss in the DSP by the name of Tomlin, who was also into the martial arts and was supposed to have had a black belt also.

The guys who knew McGrew and Tomlin often wondered who might win if the two of them were to do battle. If I remember right, McGrew's name usually was the one most of the guys picked, probably because he was a little taller than Tomlin. It didn't really matter, since no one messed with either one of them.

I found out that if you put out a little extra effort for McGrew and did a really good job, he would go out of his way to treat you really well and stick up for you if there were ever any controversies or problems with your job. I mentioned earlier that McGrew was the one who called Paul Stanley and me "The A-Team" when we were working together before I got bumped onto afternoons, so he was familiar with my work ethic, and that certainly got me off to a good start with him.

Some guys, whose reputation preceded them, were in big trouble with McGrew because he wasn't about to let anyone get the best of him. He wouldn't take any bullshit from any of them, and this often led to some pretty serious confrontations between him and some of these guys, but McGrew usually won.

Eventually, these guys would either switch with a millwright in an area who maybe wanted to work in the pool, or they would have their committeeman be on the alert for an opening in another building so that they could transfer out of the DSP.

Bill Guisi, a welder buddy of mine, was having a problem dealing with McGrew. He had only been working for him for a short time, but he could easily see that it just was not going to work out. He knew that there was going to be an opening for a welder in the Steel Division, so he set everything up with his committeeman, and the next time he had a confrontation with McGrew, which probably wasn't too long after that, he told the General to kiss his butt and then transferred out of the DSP within a few days.

I ended up working with Guisi again a few years later when I transferred to Rouge Steel and the J-9 construction area. He actually wasn't a trouble maker or anything like that, he just liked to drink a little too much, and that's what got him into trouble with McGrew.

I always kidded him when I worked with him at J-9 about it never being easy when you're working with Bill Guisi. He liked working with me because I always tried to get my job going right away so that we didn't have to fool around with it for the whole day.

We worked in some extremely nasty, hot areas in the Steel Division, and the guys did not want to spend any more time in some of those hell holes than they absolutely had to. I will talk more about this later. I think the day I told Bill I was retiring, I actually saw some tears swell up in his eyes. We definitely shared a lot of good memories.

Another millwright by the name of Mike Cleary, a hot-tempered Irishman whose nickname later became "wild child", was another good example of some of these confrontations I've talked about. He started on afternoons shortly after I did, however, he had come from another building.

Mike was about my size, maybe 5 foot 9 inches and 165 pounds, and was always clashing with McGrew over one thing or another. Mike was a good millwright and pretty much knew what he was doing, but he just did not like the General telling him what to do all the time.

One night, he and McGrew got into a real shouting match and the next day Mike did not come in. Shortly afterwards, he was gone from the Stamping Plant and ended up working at J-9 in the Steel Division, where he eventually ended up as a millwright foreman.

However, before Mike left the DSP, I got to know him fairly well, as we worked as partners quite a few times.

It turned out that he was also a cigarette boat racer. These were the long narrow boats that run on the Great Lakes. Mikes father-in-law was rather wealthy and was one of the major backers behind these races. One day while working with him, he invited me and another millwright buddy of ours, Dave D'Alfonso, to a big party that was going to help kick off the new racing year. It was held at his father-in-law's large condominium clubhouse somewhere southwest of the Detroit Metropolitan Airport.

Dave was a tall, balding guy, probably around 6 foot 3 inches and weighed maybe 175 pounds. He lived on Grosse Isle, which is a rather elegant island just southeast of the Rouge complex on the Detroit River, which is also home to the Ford Yacht Club. Dave and I had previously agreed to meet for a drink at a bar that he was familiar with, and that wasn't too far from the I-96 expressway.

Not being familiar with any of the people at this party except Mike and maybe a couple of other guys from the Rouge, we thought we had better come up with a good game plan for when we got to the clubhouse and had to deal with all of these big shooters. If I remember correctly, I think the plan was to drink more beer and try to stay as loose as possible and just mingle with everyone in the best way we could.

Actually, the party worked out better than we thought it would. We ate some good food, drank a little beer, and had some engaging conversations. Mike came around and introduced us to most of his friends and family, who ended up telling us some interesting stories about the boat racing business. A couple members of his racing team tried to recruit us to help fund some of the races. However, it didn't take them too long to figure out that skilled tradesmen at Ford could not afford to fund boat races.

All in all, we had a good time at the party, and best of all, we each managed to make it back home without encountering any problems.

Later on, that same spring, as the weather became warmer, Dave and I planned a big fishing trip in the Detroit River and Lake Erie. He had a nice fishing boat that he kept docked near his house, so we were going to meet early in the morning, load the boat up and head out for a good, relaxing, day of fishing. However, there was only one problem – my Ford van broke down about three miles from his house.

I had stopped at a party store and bought some beer, nuts, and chips and was all set to go, except that the van wouldn't co-operate. I had to call Dave and cancel our fishing trip and use my Allstate road service card to get the van and myself back to Plymouth. Just another example of what happens to the best laid plans.

The early days of working on afternoons for McGrew were very interesting, but things finally started to settle down after the first year. We had a good crew of men who all got along with each other. I was finally resigned to the fact that I was going to be stuck on afternoons for a while, and that there was nothing I could do about it, so I felt that I might as well enjoy it the best I could.

I eventually got into a card game that I had never played before called tonk. The guy's used to play this fun game at lunchtime and sometimes on our break, provided there was enough time. One of our senior millwrights, Dick Nowitzke, whose 6-foot 6 inch, 290-pound frame was difficult to miss, always seemed to be the first one at the table ready to play. He was more or less considered the leader of the pack when it came to playing this fast-flowing game and he was always hard to beat.

Another millwright who played cards with us was this funny little Italian guy by the name of Angelo. Angelo worked in an area upstairs rather than in our millwright pool and was a very good, long- time buddy of Big Dick's. When the two of them stood next to each other, they looked like the old comic strip characters Mutt and Jeff.

Al Fenech, a welder buddy of mine who usually worked in my crew, was another card player. Al was always asking me questions about our house that we built in 1985 on three acres west of Plymouth. He and his wife were preparing to do the same thing on some property that they had bought in Brighton, and they wanted to avoid many of the pitfalls that we had gone through. My wife and I were fortunate to have benefitted from the UAW legal services plan that had just come into being about the same time our house was being built.

To make a long story short, our court case against the builder of our house was still going on at the time of my retirement in 1998. It was the largest case in the approximately twelve-year history of the plan.

Still, it helped us in many ways, one of which was paying for an architect to come in and set up a working plan for the builder to make necessary repairs. However, we were unable to collect about $17,000 that was awarded us by the court. He had an excellent lawyer who bailed him out of another jam by having him file for bankruptcy – for the third time! How amazing is that? It seems really hard to believe that this guy gets to continue building houses even after he's stiffed one person after another. Maybe I shouldn't suggest this, but with what is going on in today's society with all these bribes being handed out, and taken by unscrupulous people – I wonder if someone's palm might have gotten greased in order to accomplish what that lawyer did for this guy.

Before going on, I have one more story to tell about this house-building experience. It was late October, and the roof of the house had been ready to shingle for the past three or four weeks. We had quite a bit of rain that fall, but that was no excuse for not getting the job done. There were plenty of nice days in between when the builder could have gotten a roofing crew out there to get the job done. I had talked to him several times about this, and he kept saying he was having a hard time getting guys who were covered with insurance to do the job. Finally, he and his head carpenter met at the house while I was there.

The three of us were standing in the kitchen area talking when I just had enough of his excuses and so I said, "Lets you and I go down stairs." Now I was only 5 foot 7 inches and 158 pounds. He was about 6 foot 1 inch or so and at least 230 pounds, and I was jumping up and down in his face screaming because I was tired of getting walked on by this ass hole.

He must have been quite familiar with this type of situation because he just stood there, calm as a cucumber, not letting anything I was saying bother him. I on the other hand was getting all hot and red in the face, and just about ready to blow a gasket.

Looking back at that situation now, I can laugh, but at the time, I didn't think it was so funny. Anyhow, I must have made an impression, because a day or so later, a roofing crew was out there nailing down shingles. The leader of this crew told me that the roof couldn't have taken another rain without causing a serious buckling problem. So, in a way, I felt justified in acting like I did. What an experience!

As far as I can remember, Al's house went up without too many problems. Lucky guy. There was another welder who sometimes played cards with us. He was a Middle Eastern guy whose name I believe was also Al. I didn't know him too well, until I started playing cards with him. It turned out that he was an ex-boxer, and a very good one at that. He was only about 5 foot 6 inches, but he must have weighed 180 pounds or more and had shoulders about three feet wide.

This guy was always playing the numbers, and his favorite was the four-digit pick. He spent quite a bit of money doing this, probably around $100 a week or more. Actually, I would bet that it was quite a bit more. It was no wonder he was always working so much overtime! Anyhow, he would hit for a few thousand dollars every once in a while and that would make him pretty happy. But, I remember one time when he came into our lunch room quite a bit more excited than usual because he had hit for around twelve grand on his social security number.

This was life on afternoons in the DSP, and it was around this time when I started writing poems. I must have written over seventy-five of them in a three-year period. And the one that became really well- known around the plant was "The Stamping Plant Blues." I was inspired to write this poem by a combination of several things – such as being forced to work a shift we didn't want to work, having to put up with the constant changes that supervisors were always making with our jobs, and dealing with the pressure to get important jobs done on time so that production could get up and started once again after being down for a day or so, or maybe just a matter of hours. Production was extremely important and vital to the wellbeing of the Stamping Plant.

McGrew was under a lot of pressure from his superintendent to put the heat on us to get these jobs done, so he was constantly asking us to work through our break or lunch hour so production could get up and running again. We didn't have to do it, and quite a few of the guys would not have anything to do with it and would joke about those of us who would do the work.

We were supposed to get paid when we worked through our lunch, but more often than not, we didn't. This meant that we would then have to go back to which-ever boss it was and remind him to put it in for our next check. This usually affected our take-home pay in one way or another because of the tax deductions. That's another reason why a lot of the guys just did not want to do it.

Some bosses were better than others when it came to paying us for working through our breaks or lunch, and McGrew was one of the better ones. That's one reason why we usually did it when he asked us.

Zaya, the hyper boss who got into trouble by running into people with his foreman's scooter, owed me and a good deal of others a ton of overtime hours. Because he was so bad about seeing that we were paid, we eventually quit doing it for him.

One afternoon, after getting tired of sorting out the millwrights and welders and having to take too much time to hand out all of the job assignments, McGrew brought a can of white spray paint to our meeting.

He then proceeded to paint a white line across the floor while we just stood back far out of his way with a wry smile on most of our faces. After completing the long, white line he directed the millwrights over to one side of the line and the welders to the other side. As you can probably imagine there were a lot of jokes cracked about that line. But, however, a year or so later, it was still there and being used to good effect.

After finishing my Stamping Plant poem, I showed it to some of the guys. The feedback was better than I expected as the men really liked it and suggested I type it out and give a copy to McGrew. At first, I was a little skeptical, thinking they might be just trying to get a good laugh at my expense. They did however, seem quite sincere about it so I finally sat down and typed it out. I thought that a good time to hand the poem to McGrew would be at our next safety meeting, which was held on the same Thursday night that we received our weekly paycheck. Once everyone finally arrived, I told McGrew to sit down because I had something to read. He got a weird, kind of questionable look on his face, but decided to humor me.

After moving back several steps to give myself some room, I pretended to come walking in towards the white line the same way McGrew always did, which was tugging on his dark blue baseball cap and hitching up his blue work pants. Then I proceeded to read, The Stamping Plant Blues.

The Stamping Plant Blues

Standing here in our work shoes,
Restless and edgy as the time draws near,
For the General to appear,
Man we've got the Stamping Plant Blues.

Suddenly there's a hush.
As he makes his presence felt, we all begin to melt.
Not wanting to blow his mind, we quickly come to attention,
On the right side of the line.

Walking quickly, hitching up his pants and tugging on his cap,
The General doesn't want anyone taking a nap.
Man we've got the Stamping Plant Blues.

As he gives out the jobs, we listen carefully,
Not wanting to miss a single cue,
For the General repeats to only a few.

Receiving our assignments,
We rush quickly to the job, and break out the tools,
Never wanting to look like a bunch of fools.

We know, of course, that the General will soon be making changes,
So we play the game, just to save his name.
It wouldn't be so bad, but what really makes it so sad,
Is when it's getting late and time for our break,
Which the General says we won't be able to take,

We go right on working, watching the other men smirking.
Never saying a word, we just stay true, to our fearless leader,
General Glenn T. Mc Grew.
Man, we've really got the Stamping Plant Blues.

McGrew absolutely loved this poem and carried a copy of it around in his shirt pocket to show to all of his fellow bosses and anyone else he could find to listen to it. The guys used to kid about him still carrying that poem around for a year or so later.

My buddy Al Fenech was always giving me a boost of confidence by telling me that I might have a hidden talent and that I should write more poems. Without a doubt, I owe a lot to Al for doing that because it did help me continue to write quite a few more poems. I would get ideas as we were riding around on our welding buggy going from one job to another. As I got these ideas I jotted down notes on the back of requisition cards and re-wrote them later into a poem in my spare time at home.

As a matter of fact, I still have quite a few of those original requisition cards with bits of poems written on them.

One of the few things that we had to look forward to on afternoons were the famous safety talks given by McGrew after he handed out our weekly checks. As I mentioned earlier, he was a martial arts expert, and therefore took very good care of his body, so his safety talks were quite often about healthy eating habits and getting sufficient exercise.

McGrew's lunch pail usually included carrots and celery sticks, a tomato and maybe a small can of tuna, along with some sort of fresh fruit, such as, an apple.

Can you imagine the look on the faces of a bunch of millwrights and welders when their boss is telling them about eating health food? Hell, on the day shift, it wasn't uncommon for certain guys to go out nearly every day for a burger, fries and a beer.

Some of the other things McGrew talked about were the benefits of eating 100 percent whole wheat bread and drinking skim milk, as well as eating fresh vegetables and fruit – all things I had been doing since around 1978-79 when I had to make major changes in my eating habits.

One of his best lectures was about the adverse effects of the food taste enhancer monosodium glutamate (MSG). He said that it was a common ingredient in many foods we eat, such as sausages, flavored chips, popcorn and many boxed foods. People who suffer from migraine headaches or fibromyalgia should definitely not eat any foods that have MSG in them because it can aggravate their condition and make it worse. He was using this as a good example of ingredients that are added to food that are not very good for us and that we should be aware of this. None of us need to eat any of this crap that negatively affects our body and MSG is at the top of the list. Today, high fructose corn syrup and trans fats can also be added to that list.

One afternoon, I was talking with McGrew about all of the back problems that I had in the past and he said, "Ralph, I've had some of the same problems. In fact, it got so bad that I decided to go see a chiropractor. He told me an exercise to do that really helped me and I still do it, although not as often as I should. I swear if more people knew about it, the chiropractor business would be cut in half."

McGrew walked over to an area where there was a bar made from a piece of 1 ½ inch round steel welded across an old door opening that wasn't being used any longer. He jumped up and grabbed it, saying "Here's what you have to do. Spread your hands out slightly wider than your shoulders and suspend yourself without trying to hold yourself up. Just let your weight hang freely – this is very important. Now start swinging your legs back and forth. Eventually, after building up some strength, you will be able to hold your legs out in front of you at a ninety-degree angle."

The second part of the exercise is to bring your legs up to the back of your knees and twist back and forth. These are both great exercises for strengthening your abdominal and lower back muscles as well as your arms. You can also do pull-ups or chin-ups to help strengthen your arms, if you elect.

The most important thing about doing this two-part exercise that is better than any other back exercise is that it helps realign your spine. It really works, believe me!

After seeing McGrew do this and trying it myself, I was convinced that it would not only help me, but also any of the other guys who wanted to give it a try. I ended up making a bar and some brackets and had one of our welders help me set it up.

We located it off to one side of the balcony from where we had our line-up, and just high enough so that anyone who wanted to use it could easily do so. I actually started to get up there a little earlier so that I could do my exercises before we had to leave for our job assignment. Once in a while, someone else would try it out, but unfortunately, they were never too serious about it.

I ended up doing this exercise about three or four times a week for the rest of my time on afternoons, which was three years. As a result of doing this I never had another problem with my back while working in the DSP.

One of our welders on afternoons in the DSP was a giant of a man whom I called "Billy the Kid". Bill was a very friendly guy who stood around 6 foot 2 inches and whose girth would make it difficult for two guys my size to get their arms around him.

I really liked Bill because even though he obviously had some problems doing a lot of jobs that required climbing or getting into tight spots, he never backed down from any of them. And he wasn't afraid to get all dirty and nasty if that's what it took to get the job done. Unfortunately, he often had to remain that way until the end of the shift because he never wore coveralls, only blue jeans and a t-shirt with a welder's jacket to protect his arms.

He always gave it his best shot, but occasionally we would have to bail him out if it was something such as having to reach out to burn or weld a piece of steel that was just too hard for him to reach.

After I wrote the poem, The Stamping Plant Blues, Billy was always asking me how I was doing with some of the other things that I was writing. One night, I pulled a sheet of paper out of my pocket and said, "Read this." When he finished, he looked at me and said something like, "Not bad, where did you find it?" I just said, "I've been working on it for a few days and just finished it up yesterday." Billy the Kid just shook his head like he could not believe I wrote it. Anyhow, it's called, The River, and I hope you enjoy it.

The River

The river was flowing fast, rushing across the multi-colored rocks like a runaway train, screaming out of control.

I could only wish that it would slow down, and let me come aboard, for an unforgettable ride into the vast beauty that nature has spun throughout her north woods.

Whether this would ease the pain of knowing that I will never be able to see you again I don't know.

For this is a river waiting for a fool such as I, to challenge her majestic beauty, and discover her many hidden pleasures.

Yes, this is a river that is not unlike any woman I have ever known.

This is a river that will drain you of all your strength, leaving you with an emptiness inside that makes you feel like you have lost something very close to you, that means so very much.

Something that when all is said and done will make you wish that you had never climbed aboard for that unforgettable ride. Yes, that unforgettable ride of the river.

One other poem that I wrote at this time was about the great country rebel singer Hank Williams Jr. After writing this poem called "My Name is Hank," I was able to read it to the station manager at W4 country in Detroit. He liked it quite a bit and gave me a phone number to call, that could have put me in contact with Hank's manager at the time. Unfortunately, my efforts failed to get a response and as of 2018, I'm still hoping that maybe someone like Kid Rock, who is buddies with Hank, will see this and say, "Hey, Hank needs to have a copy of this." Another poem that I wrote around this time is called "The Yee-ha Boys." I always thought that it could be turned into a song or jingle. It's something that I think Toby Keith, Willie Nelson, Hank or even Kid Rock could have a lot of fun with. Back in the day, things used to get pretty wild when we were out partying and that's what this poem is about- having fun and getting a little crazy.

My Name is Hank

Hank Jr., that's all you have to say.
Everyone knows Hank Jr.
He's come a long ways since the Ed Sullivan days.
Just a tall young cowboy on TV, singing his daddy's songs.
Now, he really knows where he belongs.

That old wooden Indian isn't quite what it used to be,
But it sounds alright to me.
He's been through some tough times down through the years,
But now he's making some great music for our ears.
Hank Jr. that's all you have to say, Hank Jr.

Lately though, Hank Jr. has had a few problems at some of his concerts and
Because of that, here's what he has to say.

My name is Hank and I've gotta get away. I've gotta, gotta, gotta, get away.

I'm running out of words to write, and songs to sing.

I don't even want to hear the telephone ring.

My rhyming ain't right and my timing is out of sync.

I guess I'll have to go out for a drink.

Then I'll be able to think

and the words will start coming,

and I'll really be humming.

Yeah, Buddy! My name is Hank, and I've gotta get away,

I've gotta, gotta, gotta, get away.

Yeah, I just have to relax my mind a little,

Because lately there's just been too much strain on the old fiddle.

Success is great, but it can also make you want to hate.

It seems like people are always tugging on me,

And expecting so much more than I can produce.

Hell, anymore, I don't even have to seduce.

Trying to keep up with the demand,

Is sometimes too much for just one man.

That's why I've gotta get away,

I've gotta, gotta, gotta, get away.

My rhyming ain't right, and my timing is out of sync.

I guess I'll have to go out for a drink.

My name is Hank.

The Yee-ha Boys

The Yee-ha boys are out on the town tonight, Yee-ha we're gonna have a good time.

When we're around the girls, we never nickel and dime it, we just big time it, pull out the dough, and let it all roll, cause we're the Yee-ha Boys, yee-ha, yeah buddy, we're gonna have one hell of a night.

There's no stopping us now, don't even try. We're gonna be cruis'n in high gear, and if you want to come along, you better be ready to kick ass and drink plenty of beer.

The Yee-ha Boys are out on the town tonight, yee-ha, were gonna have a good time.

We'll pull up to our favorite lounge in a brand new Ford F 150 4x4 truck, Don't ever have to worry about getting stuck.

Yee-ha, look out now, cause here we come, we're the Yee-ha Boys and we're ready to party.

Beer and Jack Daniels down the hatch, quarters on the pool table will never last.

Dollar in the juke- box, a couple more beers, my God the girls they all look like foxes in here.

Yee-ha, yeah buddy! The Yee-ha Boys are out on the town tonight. My last year on afternoons was spent working once again with Robbie, who was my partner when I first started working as an apprentice in the Stamping Plant. This time however, we were both journeyman millwrights and working as part of a two- man crew. Our main job each day was to inspect the various overhead cranes in the building and make any necessary repairs without having to shut the crane down for an extended period of time. This was particularly important if there was a major breakdown on one of the busiest cranes in the plant. Whenever this would happen, the heat would really be on us big time to get that bad boy back running up and down the aisles again as soon as possible.

Several years earlier, a millwright, whose name was Luzinski and another millwright whose name I can't remember, did this job. They, however, both transferred to the Steel Division so that they could make more money by working overtime and getting large incentive bonuses that were gauged on the amount of steel that the building made for that particular week.

Robbie was then given the job because McGrew didn't want him on the floor any longer because he was rather lazy. So McGrew preferred to have him upstairs on the crane balcony where he actually did a pretty good job of organizing things. However, whenever there were major breakdowns and a little hustle was needed, he mostly stood or sat around with a cigarette in his hand, which, used to drive me crazy. I would be busting my butt doing most of the work as fast as I could because it was extremely hot up on those cranes, especially in the summer, and no one wanted to be up there any longer than necessary.

McGrew had previously pared different millwrights with Robbie, but they didn't last too long. My buddy, Dave, worked with him for a while and kept telling me that Robbie was really getting on his nerves and that he couldn't deal with him any longer. Dave was finally able to transfer out of the DSP and into another building, which high seniority workers could do by putting a bid in for a particular job once it was posted.

This was when McGrew decided to put me up there with Robbie, hoping that I could deal with him better than the other guys were able to do. Well, it wasn't easy, but I managed to hang around for nearly a year or so with Robbie on the crane balcony.

Most of our time during the week was spent inspecting cranes. We would try to take one before lunch and one after, picking one that had not been done yet that particular week and one that was not being used for a while. We usually checked with the crane operator to make sure we were both on the same page as far as how long we could have the crane tied up for the inspections.

We were in a kind of quiet spot up there, and as long as we did our job and kept the cranes running, management didn't mess with us too much. They knew how hot it was up on the cranes and that we earned our money when we were working on a breakdown.

I was going thru some poems the other day that I had written while working in the DSP and found this one that I had forgotten about and had dedicated to Robbie while I was working with him on the crane balcony. He was always telling me about his girlfriend and how she always seemed to want this or that from him, or how she wanted him to do things with her that he did not particularly want to do. Robbie was probably seven or eight years younger than me and was rather immature with a bad attitude about women. He liked them and wanted to be with them for all the good things, but then that was it. He did not want any part of all that other stuff. So, consequently, I got tired of all his pouting and hearing his stories about putting women down and therefore I wrote this poem as a joke.

She's My Woman

She's my woman and that's all I want her to be,
I said, can't you see, that's all I want her to be.
She's my woman.

I'm not asking for a lot,
I just want her to keep my bed hot.
She's my woman.

Take her out, sit down and talk?
I'll only pout. Go for a walk? Are you kidding?
Who's got time? I've got to drink some more wine.
She's my woman, and all I want is for her to keep my bed hot.
She's my woman.

Every time I get some money, she starts calling me honey.
Honey take me here, honey take me there.
You're such a sweet thing, why don't you buy me a diamond ring?
She's my woman.

What more could I expect?
Except to write another check.
She's my woman.

It seems she's never satisfied until it's all gone,

And leaves me feeling just like a pawn.

This is my woman and that's all I want her to be?

Now you see why all I want is for her to keep my bed hot,

And thanks a lot, I said, thanks a lot, cause she's my woman.

One week while Robbie was on vacation, McGrew sent a millwright by the name of Jeff upstairs to work with me. I had known Jeff, who was a white guy about my size, for some time and so therefore, I felt reasonably comfortable with him. However, Jeff had a problem with height that he failed to tell McGrew about.

When he told me this I said, "Don't worry, I'll go up on the crane and do the inspections. It will take a little longer, but we'll work it out. You can be the safety watch while I'm up there."

Well, this worked alright until one day while doing the inspections I found a bunch of bolts sheared off on one of the couplings connecting the main drive shaft. I climbed back down the rungs of the long, winding, steel staircase and told Jeff what I had found, and that I was going to need some help.

He said that he would try and do it, so we let McGrew know what we had found and then shut the crane down so that no-one could use it by locking out the power system with our safety locks. We then drove back to the crane balcony to get all of the tools we needed, which also gave me some time to discuss the job with Jeff and, hopefully, let his nerves settle down.

It only took us a short while to get everything we needed and drive back to the tall staircase that had safety rings around it and was probably fifty feet high or higher. I went up first and set my tool pouch off to the side and watched while Jeff began to climb up the same spiral, staircase. Because of safety reasons, one worker doesn't start climbing up a staircase like this until the other one is completely off of it.

Anyhow, Jeff managed to get maybe halfway up the staircase at the most when he froze. He stayed there for a minute or so, but just could not make it any further. I yelled back down to him to just be careful and get back to the ground floor, which he was finally able to do. We eventually got some more help over there and had the crane running once again before too real long – another job well done! But not without some excitement.

As an apprentice, I had heard stories about guys freezing at heights like this, who actually had to have their fingers pried off of whatever it was that they were hanging on to. Now, I had firsthand knowledge of seeing nearly the exact same thing. I definitely felt kind of sorry for Jeff because I knew he was really embarrassed, but things like that happen sometimes in the skilled trades. Fortunately, no one was hurt, except for maybe a bruised ego. The job was safely completed and everything worked out ok.

Not too long after that, my breaking point came while McGrew was on vacation. This happened because the previously mentioned millwright, Luzinski transferred back into the Stamping Plant from the steel division, and was told he could have his old job back on the crane balcony, which meant that I would be the odd man out. Now, it did not exactly break my heart knowing that I wasn't going to be working with Robbie any longer. But, what really pissed me off, was the fact that the general foreman at the time, had no clue as to how many times I had bailed his butt out by working extra hard to get major breakdowns completed, such as, the one I just mentioned with Jeff, while Robbie didn't do didley squat.

There's no question that Luzinski was very good with the cranes, and I know that's why the general foreman wanted him back up there. However, he could have said something to me about appreciating everything that I had done. If he had done that I probably would have been satisfied and been willing to go back to the millwright pool, where I actually preferred working anyhow. Instead, he just handed him my job and never said one word to me, which as an ordinary general foreman, I guess I shouldn't have expected anything different. On the other hand, a good general foreman who knew his men and what they did for him would have come over and thanked me for a job well done.

It seemed like every time the company made a foreman or general foreman out of someone who wasn't a millwright or welder, they didn't pan out real well, and he was certainly no exception to this rule.

So, instead of waiting for McGrew to come back from vacation and straighten everything out, I was so upset because of the lack of respect he gave me that I went up to the second-floor offices and right up to his desk. And then, right in front of all his peers, I let him have it with both barrels. Talk about committing career suicide! But, that's just the way I was back then. I thought he was an asshole, and I let him know it in no uncertain terms.

McGrew could only shake his head when he came back. He actually thought it was kind of funny. He said I should have just gone along with it until he got back and then he would have made everything alright. I said, "I know Glenn, but I was so upset because I was the one who hustled and saw that the jobs got completed. He either didn't realize this or just did not care." McGrew said, "I know how you feel and I do not blame you for being upset, but there's nothing I can do for you now." I said, "That's alright. I'm happy to be back in our millwright pool. I know you appreciated what I did and that's good enough for me."

McGrew wasn't exactly exempt from all the stress and strain that was going on in the plant on afternoons either. He was having quite a few problems with his wife when they decided to split up. And, as the song goes, "He got the shaft and she got the gold mine". He had a cabin somewhere up north that he enjoyed retreating to. It was a place where he could get out and shoot his guns and just kick back and relax. We used to joke about this all the time, saying something like he probably went through a thousand rounds or more of ammunition while he was up there.

To extract revenge for something he had done either just before or after the divorce, his wife made a trip to the cabin, unbeknownst to McGrew, and messed it up pretty good. She ended up spray painting the walls and also tearing curtains up and destroying most everything that she could. I don't remember just exactly when this happened, but I do remember McGrew being in a real ugly mood one particular day and getting on my butt about something that happened on a job that he had sent me to check out.

I went over to where the job was and talked to the area boss about it. We discussed what needed to be done and when I could come back and do it without having to shut the line down. There was nothing else I could do at that particular time, so I went back to where the rest of my regular crew was working.

A few minutes later, here comes Mc Grew riding up like gangbusters and just taking off on me. His face got all beet red while he was screaming and hollering like a complete idiot. I just stood there until he was finished and then I had my say. I told him something like, "I worked it out with the production boss, and further- more, if you want to scream and holler at someone and act like a maniac, go home and yell at your wife, but don't be giving me any of that crap, because I'm not going to put up with it." Then I just walked away and went back to what I was doing before he came around.

McGrew left and then came back a little later after talking with the same production boss and apologized for acting so crazy. I accepted his apology and just said something about knowing that he was having some outside problems and that it wasn't easy when things are going bad at home.

At this point. I want to close the doors to the DSP by including another poem about McGrew and our afternoon shift that I wrote after leaving the plant. It's one of my favorite poems and one that I wrote as sort of a joke. It wasn't meant to be taken seriously. Actually, I think someone like Kid Rock could probably do a good rap tune with this:

The General's Boys

Play all day, work all night, everyone knew we were the General's Boy's. Always trying to do things right, we worked harder than all the rest, just so the General could say, he had the best.

Yeah, lots of noise, little joy. No one dared fool around with the
General's Boys.
No one dared fool around with the General's Boys.
Raising hell and kicking ass, we never let anyone bother us, especially the
top brass.
Coming into work was sometimes quite a chore.
But, working for the General always kept things from becoming a bore.
Yeah, lots of noise, little joy. Everyone knew we were the General's Boys.
Everyone knew we were the General's Boys. Giving it all we had,
sometimes wasn't good enough. So, the General would say, "Men, you just
have to get tough."
Yeah, he was quite a trip, and really knew how to get the most out of
his men,
Especially, when he would stare at them with his ice cold, steely eyes,
Crack his big old leather whip and say, "Ok men, lets get it going, knock
this job out and don't be giving me any alibis."

Yeah, the General was known to shoot from the hip and most of us knew
better than to be giving him any lip.
But, there was always someone who would do or say something at the
wrong time, and then all hell would break loose, and the General would
blow his mind, and start screaming and yelling, while we just stood
back and waited for him to cool off, knowing everything would soon be
forgotten, especially after we knocked out the job really quick, and made
it all look, like it was some kind of trick, which the General really loved.
Yeah buddy, everyone knew we were the General's Boys. Everyone knew
we were the General's Boys. Yee Ha!!
I spent a few more weeks in the DSP, but things were getting worse as far as
high seniority millwrights and welders returning from the Steel Division.
This was pretty much typical in the other buildings, such as: The Glass,
Engine, Frame and Assembly Plants.

Our union committee men were coming around all the time asking guys like myself, who they knew were on the bubble as far as seniority went, if we wanted to transfer to what was now going to be called Rouge Steel.

They continually repeated that all we needed to keep our Ford rights in case something happened at Rouge Steel, (such as, if it was sold) was a total of sixty points, which consisted of a combination of our age and our seniority, and which I easily had.

There was never any mention of any restrictions or anything else that would cause us to question a move to Rouge Steel. The reason I am mentioning this now is because of what happened some years later when one of our millwrights who was in the same group of guys that transferred as myself decided to retire and soon found out he wasn't going to be getting a full Ford retirement. This was totally contrary to what the union reps had told us. Apparently, there was a restriction that applied to people who transferred to Rouge Steel after a certain date in the fall of 1989. Again, our union never mentioned this restriction to any of us. I'm sure that if we had known about this, none of us would have made the decision to transfer from Ford. Someone should have been held responsible for this blunder, but amazingly, they never were.

Finally, an opportunity in the Assembly Plant came up for me to get out of the Stamping Plant and off of afternoons, which I absolutely needed to do. My girls were at the age where they were starting to get involved in sports, and I wanted to be there for them.

At this particular time in 1989, the Mustang was the only car being fabricated in the Dearborn Assembly Plant, and during the short time that I spent there, I was inspired to write a poem called The Mustang. I thought it would be a good introduction for this chapter on the Assembly Plant. I had given a copy of the poem to the editors of the plant's monthly paper. They liked it quite a bit and decided to use it in their May 11, 1990 edition.

The Mustang

Wild and free,
Running through the hills and trees, Mustangs seldom have time to relax,
Because they are always being driven to the max.

Strong, powerful and very sleek,
The Mustang is definitely not one for the very meek.

You see the Mustang is a wild and free spirit,
Waiting to be driven,
If you've got what it takes to get near it.

Yes, a real man is what it takes,
Because the Mustang make few mistakes.

It is one of the truly great creatures of our time,
And is always looking really fine.

So, come on, hop aboard and take a ride.
See what it's like on this animal's hide.

But, be sure and strap yourself in,
Before you get ready to take it for a spin.
Then you won't have to worry,
About getting bucked off,
And thrown into the wind.

CHAPTER 13

Life after the DSP

I was fairly familiar with the Assembly Plant because during my last year on afternoons in the previously mentioned DSP, I had spent some time over there on a few occasions to work overtime on the weekends. Mainly doing preventive maintenance (P&M) on overhead conveyor lines.

The reason for all this OT was because, earlier in the year, a worker was either severely injured or killed when some of the bolts sheared off of the hangers on these conveyor lines that were carrying motors and fenders, causing them to come tumbling down.

Once again, it took a horrible accident to get the company to establish a full- time preventive maintenance program in an effort to avert things, such as this, from ever happening again. Unfortunately, it always seemed to work this way.

My new partner was Tom Czarnomski, a fellow Polish guy with a big bushy beard who I had known from when he worked in the DSP several years earlier. He and I worked together for about six months on midnights doing P&M work on the overhead conveyors. We then got bumped onto days for a few weeks until we decided to make a big life changing move of transferring to the Steel Division. We felt that we had to make this move because we were not getting enough OT and because we could both pretty much pick our shift, which for the both of us was extremely important.

We had attended several union meetings and talked with our committeeman, George Snow, and we were always told we would have a full Ford retirement whenever we elected to retire because we both met all the requirements. This, as I mentioned earlier, was sixty points or better based on our age (we were both over forty), plus our number of years at Ford (we both had over twenty years). Never, ever was anything said about any kind of restriction or date deadline – never! We didn't think we had to question our committeemen in regards to all of this because that was their job – to know what was going on and to keep us properly informed so that we could make the right decision for our-selves and our families. Unfortunately, that wasn't the case and we ended up getting the royal shaft.

So anyhow, Rouge Steel needed good, young, experienced millwrights, and they were practically begging us to transfer. Finally, they came up with an incentive plan that included something like $14,000 to be paid out over a year's time. Again, the committeemen were constantly hounding us and setting up meetings to explain what it all encompassed.

So, after several tension filled days of discussing all the pros and cons with our families, we decided to make the big, career altering move. Here's an excellent example of how much stress we were under at the time. One day on my way home from work, I had all these decisions that I had to make running through my mind and therefore I was not concentrating on the road ahead of me the way I should have been.

I was completely distracted by some construction work that was going on near the side of Rotunda Drive, which was the road that I used to get to the Southfield Freeway. The next thing I knew, I had run into the rear end of a large pickup truck that was being driven by the son of a millwright I knew who used to work in the Stamping Plant, Frank Driscoll.

Fortunately, no one was injured. The kid was happy because his good looking, Ford truck didn't even have a scratch on it. I, however, could not say the same about my brand new, shiny red, 1989 Tempo which ended up with a broken grill and a damaged radiator. I told him who I was and apologized for being so careless, telling him I had been under a lot of stress lately because of what was going on at work. He said that he completely understood because his Dad was in a similar situation. He was very good about it, wished me good luck and then got into his hot looking machine and drove off.

I, however, was ticketed by the officer who came to the scene for not having my car under control. I also ended up having to call a tow truck to come and pick up my car because it was un-drivable, and then called my wife so that she could come and get my butt.

To make matters even more complicated, my friend Tom nearly backed out of the move because of the fact that he would have to shave his full beard that he was extremely proud of and that he had been grooming for the last fifteen years, as a requirement to pass the respirator test in order to be accepted into Rouge Steel. I also had a small beard at the time, but didn't really mind shaving it off. Tom, however, was totally bummed out about it.

I remember him telling me something like, "Ralph, I'm just about ready to tell them to shove it." I just told him, "Tom, you will be able to grow it back and they won't do a thing about it. Guys over there have beards every bit as big as yours. Don't let it hold you back."

This all took place in the morning after our physical. The respirator test was to come in the afternoon and they warned us that in order to pass that test we would definitely have to shave.

I didn't want to drive the thirty miles back to Plymouth where my house was just to shave so I drove over to a party store and bought some shaving cream and a bag of throw away razors and then went back to the Assembly Plant and hacked the beard off.

Tom, on the other hand, decided to go home which was about fifteen miles away. Before leaving he said he was not sure if he was coming back. We had to be back to the plant by 1pm so there wasn't going to be a lot of time to procrastinate. I was sitting in the waiting room area when Tom finally showed up. I hardly recognized him. He said his wife cut it down close for him and then he shaved. They videotaped the whole process!

With clean faces, we were able to easily pass the test and get the go-ahead to start working at Rouge Steel. Tom was to start at J-9 in the mill-wright pool working days. I had enough seniority to get into a higher incentive building, the Electric Arc Furnace. This was quite important because the base pay for us was quite a bit less than we were making at Ford at the time. But, with the higher incentive from the Electric Arc, it made my total hourly pay equivalent to what I received at Ford.

Also, and this was important, there was a lot more OT nearly everywhere at Rouge Steel, and I ended up working just about as much as I could handle. My wife, Debbie, was a registered nurse at St. Mary's Hospital in Livonia, so there was no need to over-do the amount of hours I worked, as some guys did, but I still worked my share of hours.

The intense heat and the never-ending noise around the two furnaces on the second floor, especially when they were both running at the same time, was something you could never get used to. It was way louder than anything that I had ever heard before. Fortunately, the majority of the time, only one furnace ran, but occasionally the demand for our steel would be way up and so then they would have to fire up both furnaces at the same time.

Both furnaces running at the same time were unbelievably loud and whenever we had to go up there while they were running like that, I always wore both my ear plugs and my over the head earmuffs. Fortunately, we didn't have to go near those bad boys too often while they were running. Most of the work we did around them was while they were shut down and cooling off. The rest of the time, we did project work and other maintenance repairs that could be done on the ground floor away from the furnaces. Things such as repairing holes or cracks in the huge ladles that held the red-hot molten steel that was transported from one area to another by giant ladle haulers. These haulers were so huge the tires on them must have measured three feet wide and eight or ten feet high, or higher.

I felt fairly comfortable right from the beginning working in the Electric Arc Furnace because I was familiar with quite a few of the millwrights who had previously worked in the DSP. Guys such as: Henry Horn, Fred Goroni, Glen Breeding, and Terry Szarbo, who always seemed to be working with Glen. There was another millwright there that I worked with in the DSP by the name of Getts, who was a good worker, but a difficult guy to get along with. It seemed he was always saying or doing something that would get people pissed off. He was the kind of guy that really gets on your nerves.

I made an honest effort to get along with him most of the time, but it wasn't easy. One week we were forced to work through our Christmas holiday vacation for three days. Getts, who was about my size, and I were partners working high up on the crane rails doing some repair work.

It was the second day and we were both probably a little ticked off that we were being forced to work through our holiday vacation time. I cannot remember exactly what happened, but it seemed like one thing had led to another, and therefore, we weren't exactly happy campers up there working together. He ended up saying something that really upset me and I finally cracked and let him have it back. We ended up airing everything out, and after that day we got along fairly well. It's amazing how things like that can work out for the best once everything is just laid out on the table like that and there is a mutual understanding

Unfortunately, Getts was one of the millwrights injured during the disastrous Power House blowup in February of 1999.

I recently spoke with a millwright buddy of mine, who I mentioned earlier in the book, and who is now retired and living in the Naples, Florida, area. He said that the last thing he heard about Getts was that he received a million dollar settlement as a result of that tragic accident, and that he is not working anymore. Why would he? It's probably a miracle that he survived, and I certainly wish him and his family the very best of luck.

The Power House accident happened only about six weeks or so after I retired at the end of 1998. Without a doubt I consider myself extremely fortunate because I could easily have been one of those guys who was severely injured. Actually, I could have been severely injured many times while working at Ford and Rouge Steel, but it seemed I always had someone up above watching over me. There is certainly no question in my mind that I dodged my share of bullets while working in the Rouge and for that I am absolutely grateful.

Before I retired, I warned quite a few of the new young gun millwrights, as well as some of my old buddies, about the fact that there had not been a major accident in nearly two years, and that the old Rouge was about due for something bad to happen. I remember telling them to be very careful and to watch out for themselves and their partner. Unfortunately, it made me seem like a profit when that accident occurred.

Too often, when the guys have been working long hours without a lot of sleep, their bodies tend to break down, which keeps them from concentrating and focusing on the job at hand. This then leads to injuries that could have been prevented if the workers were not sleep-deprived from working so much OT.

Here's a perfect example of what not getting enough sleep and rest can do to your body. Around the spring of 1992, I was working the day shift and doing a lot of overtime in an area of Rouge Steel known as J-9. It was just before the start of our morning shift. I was in our locker room sitting on a bench, near my locker, bending over tying up my work shoes, when all of a sudden, my back tightened up. It turned out to be a very bad muscle spasm that froze me right up. I could barely move.

Somehow, I eventually was able to make it to our coffee shop, where we always met for our daily assignments and waited until my boss got there. Needless to say, the men were getting on me pretty good because of all the fresh fruit and vegetables that I used to eat all the time. They joked that if I ate more meat, I would not have so many problems. At least it got everyone laughing except myself. I was in too much pain and in a bad mood because of what happened.

When my boss, the Cat Man, came in, he could easily see that I would have to go to Central Medical. He got on his phone and called the van that they use to take patients to and from the medical center and, within a short time, I was sitting in the center waiting to see a doctor. Fortunately, I didn't have to wait too long. The reason I say that is because anyone who has ever been over there before knows that they would be lucky to get in to see someone in less than an hour. It was ridiculous how long it took sometimes. This was one of the big reasons bosses dreaded sending people over there for only mild problems. They knew they would be lucky to see them again before a couple hours or so.

The doctor I saw prescribed 800 mg of Motrin, Flexeral, a strong muscle relaxer, and also some Tylenol #3 to use if the pain got really bad. No exercise was prescribed.

I had to return the next day for another examination. This time, however, a different doctor came into the room to see me. After thoroughly checking me out he decided to keep me off work for a week or so.

All of this was very frustrating for me because I felt so damn helpless. The medication, especially the Flexeral kept me feeling drowsy, so I ended up sleeping for two or three hours each afternoon. This was the first time in about six years or more that I had experienced any trouble with my back.

I absolutely believe that one of the main reasons for this was that I had been doing the special hanging exercises that I mentioned previously, which kept my back and abs firm and strong. However, since transferring to Rouge Steel, I had become a little lax in doing them and unfortunately, it cost me.

This just shows how doing a task as simple as tying your shoes can cause a medical problem when you haven't been getting enough rest.

Double shifts in the Steel Division were quite common at this time and believe me a lot of guys were working them. That, of course, is why they transferred - to work the OT and make big bucks. I did not realize how much working all of those doubles affected my health until after I retired and started to get a good night's sleep in my own bed rather than on a bench in a locker room. It was no wonder that I ended up having to retire because of all the restrictions I was on during my last year at the Rouge.

My body wasn't able to hold up due to a combination of things, such as a lack of sleep and too much OT. As a result, I was overly susceptible to injuries, especially to my back and my shoulders, which were two of the most common injuries for millwrights.

Nearly all millwrights have major back problems and have had one or both shoulders operated on by the time they have been a journeyman for twenty or thirty years, and I was no exception.

So, when I first heard about the explosion in the Power House, I was not totally surprised, but I was still very upset. It bothered me a lot because I knew how old everything was over there in that area and that danger was lurking around every corner.

There were definitely some exciting moments in the Electric Arc. One night, my good buddy Henry Horn and another millwright were taking the delta out of the roof of one of the furnaces with an overhead crane. As they were slowly putting pressure on the cables of the crane to pull the delta out (evidently it was extremely tight and causing them all kinds of problems), it broke loose and knocked them over and up against the super structure of the roof. It ended up breaking the other millwright's arm and cracked a couple of Henry's ribs. He was injured bad enough to be hospitalized for a week or more. I talked to him after he got out and he said they were very fortunate that it wasn't a lot worse. So, without a doubt, this was just another excellent example of how fast things can go wrong while working in an extremely dangerous environment, such as we had to do so very often at Rouge Steel.

The standard procedure for doing this dangerous job was to take the delta out while the roof was off of the furnace sitting safely on the floor somewhere. Occasionally, however, for one reason or another, there would be exceptions to this rule.

The delta is a large, brick ring that fits into an opening in the furnace roof and is about six or seven feet in diameter. There is some ductwork that connects to this when the superstructure of the roof is swung into its final position. A strong blower then forces the poisonous exhaust fumes and smoke through this ductwork and eventually into another building called the "bag house," where it is stored in long, narrow bags until an outside firm comes in and vacuums it out.

Speaking of the bag house, one of the least desirable jobs for the millwrights in the Electric Arc was to change these bags once they were worn out. Everyone sort of held their breath when that job was being assigned because it was nothing but a very nasty, dirty job that no one wanted any part of.

In the Steel Division, just about any job in any one of the buildings was far worse than anywhere in the production buildings at Ford's, hands down no comparison.

Here is another excellent example of how danger can be lurking around the corner at just about any time. One day my boss sent me upstairs to help two other millwrights who were having some difficulty taking a furnace door off of one of the two furnaces, so that the inside walls could be re-lined with new firebrick.

They were experiencing some problems with getting the heavy, cumbersome door hooked up because the overhead crane cables were not able to come straight down to the door. The roof of the furnace had a slight overhang to it, so we had to reach over and pull the heavy cables back into the door, which made the job quite a bit more difficult. Another road block that acted as a hindrance to accomplishing this job was the fact that there was a hole in the floor, approximately 2 1/2 by 4 feet, directly below the door. This was used for pouring molten steel into an empty ladle sitting directly below on the ground floor.

The safe way to do this difficult job was to cover this hole with safety planks and plywood, but sometimes, when the guys couldn't find a piece of plywood to put over the boards, they would just use the safety planks. There were some guys that would not do this job unless that hole was completely covered, but then there were other guys who would, and this particular night, they only had planks across the hole.

I knew that this wasn't the safest way to do the job, but they already had the crane set up to pull the door out, (Once a crane is in position to do a job you better have everything in order because once it leaves you might have to wait forever to get it back.) so consequently, I just tried to be very careful. What I did not know, however, and what they failed to tell me, was that the safety latch or bolt on this door, which was supposed to be pulled out last, after the cables were hooked up and ready to pull the door out, had already been taken out before I got up there.

This was a big no-no, and so as I reached across the hole to make the last connection to the crane, the tension from the crane caused the door to come swinging out away from the furnace, which in turn loosened some of the firebrick that the planks were sitting on, causing them to spread out a little, which, in turn, caused me to lose my balance and slip and fall feet-first into the hole. Fortunately, the only thing that saved me was that I was able to get my elbows on each side of the boards to support myself until those two guys could grab a hold of my arms and pull me back up and out of that harrowing situation. Whew!!! If I had fallen all the way through that hole, I would have ended up in the empty, but still hot ladle directly below me, and it more than likely would have been adios amigo.

This was just another excellent example of being assigned to a job that someone else had started, and trying to help out, only to end up almost losing my life because someone else had decided to take a short cut in doing their job. Not good! Now, you might reasonably say, "Why then did you not refuse to do the job as it was set up?" I proceeded to do the job because I knew there was no time to waste. The crane operator had other jobs to do and the brick layers were ready to start the re-lining job. They did have the hole covered with safety planks as I stated, and guys have done that job like that before. It's not like it was the first time someone had stepped on only those planks.

So, the decision was made to go ahead and do it. Unfortunately, while on the midnight shift guys often end up taking short cuts for various reasons. They could be working a double shift and want to get the job finished up and get out of there as soon as possible. They don't want to end up being on a job any longer than they possibly have to. One other factor is that there isn't as many white shirts walking around all over the place as there is on days. So, they go ahead and cheat a little, thinking everything will be alright. And it usually was ok. However, as in this case, shit happens and it nearly resulted in a tragic accident.

One evening while working in the Electric Arc, I remember having an engaging conversation with a young black millwright. We were talking about black guys cheating on their women. He was saying something about the fact that black women tend to expect this from their men. They might not like it, but they just feel that that's the way they are, and that they don't think that it's that big of a deal. Hum, if they don't think it is that big of a deal, then why are there so many single, black mother's out there? Aren't they the ones who get tired of their men cheating on them?

He then went on to tell me about why he thought so many black guys prefer white women. According to him it was because they get tired of the black women's attitude. I'll just pass on that statement.

Sometime after 1992, the Electric Arc Furnace, to my dismay, went down to a skeletal crew for a year or so and then eventually shut down completely. The majority of the skilled tradespeople, including myself, went back to the J-9 construction area in the old Rolling Mill. I was upset about this because of the high incentive pay that we would be losing. However, I certainly would not miss all of that deafening noise.

I knew all about J-9 and all of the various jobs that they did throughout the Rouge Steel area. At this particular time, there must have been around forty millwrights and fifteen to twenty welders working out of this area, doing these jobs in and around the mill and also doing breakdowns and weekend repairs at the "Hot Strip," which was our main customer. It seemed as though we were always over there doing something because their millwrights just did the everyday jobs on the main floor where the steel was rolled out. J-9 did just about everything else.

After working midnights and making the high incentive money at the Electric Arc, I wasn't satisfied with making less money at J-9 and having to work days. So, I decided to take a job that opened up in the Hot Strip on midnights. I would be rebuilding work rolls and doing other maintenance work in that area. Desperation can make us do some crazy things, such as not taking the good advice of my good buddy Fred Goroni and welder Bill Geisi who both warned me not to take that job. They knew what it was like over there, especially Fred who had done that job several years earlier before giving it up because it was too rough on his body. He was about 6 foot 2 inches tall and around 215 pounds, compared to my 5-foot 7-inch, 158-pound frame.

I, of course, had to be bull-headed and find out for myself. I had always kept my body in good physical condition, and even though I was starting to have some shoulder problems, I thought I could handle whatever they had to throw at me. What a miscalculation that turned out to be.

I could see from the very first night on those work rolls, which were approximately 24 to 30 inches in diameter and 10 to 12 feet or longer, that I wasn't going to like anything about them. The whole sequence seemed too much like production work.

I had to climb up a short set of steps to get on a sliding platform, which was probably about 6-foot or so off the ground floor.

An overhead crane would bring these large steel rollers down and set them across a work area, where I had a ratchet to loosen the bolts on the huge bearings at the end of each of these rollers and also a pry bar and sometimes a sledge hammer to help slide these bearings off of the "work rolls" as they were called.

The biggest problem for me was that at my height, most of the work that I had to do was at shoulder level. And so, by the end of the shift, after doing anywhere between twelve and twenty–four of these rolls (twelve to seventeen wasn't too bad of a night, but seventeen to twenty–four was a pretty rough night), I was totally wiped out. This was especially true if the old bearings did not come off without a struggle, and too often this was the case.

I was trying diligently to hang in there and learn how to do this miserable job so it wouldn't be so tough, but my shoulders, especially my right one (I'm right-handed) were beginning to bother me more and more.

Our bosses tended to alternate from shift to shift, and for the most part, were quite good and understanding with someone new to this particular type of work, with one exception. A short, stocky, balding guy who was nothing but a plain and simple jerk and a poor excuse for a boss. That's not to say he wasn't smart, maybe he was actually too smart for his own good, but no matter, he was still a jerk never the less.

He had been giving this one old rigger a hard time for quite a while, and finally the old boy had enough and decided to retire, but not before filing and winning a grievance against him.

The reason that I am mentioning this is because this same guy had been giving me a hard time also. He wanted me to work faster and get more work rolls done in a shorter amount of time, which was what I was striving to do. I tried to explain that I was having some problems with my shoulder, but he would have nothing to do with it. In fact, he would try and get cute and make stupid little jokes, which were funny only to him. Anyhow, his last little joke is what caused my downfall at the mill and, by the way, eventually led to his dismissal as a boss.

This one particular night was a very tough one, with about nineteen to twenty rolls that needed to be changed, many of which were very difficult to get the huge, heavy bearings off, and so by the end of the shift, I was totally wiped out.

I was working a double shift that day, however, so I only had time for a short break before the day shift started up.

Now the way they nearly always worked this, was when a guy was going to work a double, he would get a different, less physical job for the day shift if he had worked the work rolls on the previous shift. To my dismay, however, the boss on days this particular morning was this same ass hole, and when he saw that I was working over he decided to get cute and said something about me needing to get some more time in on working those rolls, even though he knew we had just gone through a tough midnight shift. So, he had me do another shift on that same job.

Right there I should have declined to do it and just told him I was going home. If I had been working there for a year or so I definitely would have done that. However, I was still rather new in the plant and didn't want to make any waves. I still wanted to be able to work doubles and didn't want to get anyone pissed off, so I worked the shift and didn't complain about it.

Well, as it turned out, the day shift was even worse than midnights. I must have done twenty-two to twenty-three or more of those rolls, and by the time the day shift was over, I was hurting big time. After stripping my cloths off in our locker room I stood under a hot shower for the longest time trying to sooth my aching muscles. This helped a little, but I was so bad off that I could hardly dress myself.

After returning to my house that afternoon, I took some Motrin that I had and laid down to get some well- deserved sleep so I could go back to work that same evening for the start of my regular shift. I slept quite well, but upon waking up, I could barely move my arms, especially my right one, which I couldn't even hold up for more than a few seconds.

I then got on the phone and left a message with the clerk that I was not going to be able to work that night because of what happened the previous night and day, and that I would be going in to Central Medical at work the next morning.

At Central Med., I explained to the doctor exactly what happened the previous night and day. I told him that I was having some problems with my shoulder bothering me before this, but that I was doing OK until they overloaded me.

The doctor sounded rather upset and wanted to know the name of the boss who ordered me to do the same difficult job while doing a double shift. I didn't hesitate to tell him who it was. It did not surprise me one bit at all when he seemed to recognize the name, probably because there were other complaints about him. Anyhow, he gave me some muscle relaxers and wrote out a work restriction.

I don't remember all the details about what happened after that, except that the Hot Mill could no longer use me with the work restrictions, and because I was on loan from J-9, they sent me back there.

A couple months or so later, if that long, this man, who was such a poor excuse for a boss, was sent packing back to his previous job in the Cold Mill, which I believe was as a machine repairman. I ended up settling in at J-9, but was limited in what I could do. After months of nonproductive physical therapy, I had arthroscopic surgery on my right shoulder in the fall of 1992, and then in the spring of 1993 I had to have neck surgery as a result of a pinched nerve I acquired after a bad bout of sneezing from a sinus cold.

In all, I was off work for over a year and went through months of agonizing physical therapy. When I finally returned to work, I was healthy and strong and able to work enough OT to keep me satisfied at J-9.

Although my stay in the Hot Mill was rather short, it did provide me with another good story about a little machine repairman by the name of Danny. Danny was a wild eyed, hyper guy who reminded me a lot of Charles Manson. He also happened to be a crack cocaine addict. Even so, he was a smart, good worker, that is when he was at work. "At work" are the key words here, because we would never know when he would go off on a binge. He would be doing really well for several weeks and then have a long weekend off and come back all messed up, if he even came back at all. He used to tell me stories about him and his biddies stripping metal off of buildings and re-selling it to get money to buy their crack.

Another thing they did was to go into a Sears store and walk out with boxes of tools right in front of a salesperson. The salesperson had to call security, and by then, they would be gone. Quite often, however, they would be identified by surveillance cameras and picked up shortly afterwards. Amazing!

One of the last times I talked with Danny was after he came back from one of his four- day binges and, according to him, he had not slept in three days. He also told me that he had not used crack in more than eight weeks before this, so he decided to do it up really good. I tended to believe him because he was absolutely flying – wild eyed and screaming and hollering.

He then showed me his nylon jacket that had stains all over it, which he said came from having sex with a woman he met in a crack house that he had been hanging around. I just shook my head in amazement. I really liked Danny and hoped he was able to overcome this awful addiction. The company and union had special programs set up for guys that were having problems with drugs or alcohol, so at least he was given a chance to make it back to living a normal life.

CHAPTER 14

Tragedy Strikes and a Lesson Learned

When the weekends rolled around, we would quite often have guys on our midnight shift that did not normally work the graveyard shift, as it was called. One particular night, we had a couple of journeymen millwrights and some apprentices join us for a couple of big jobs that were scheduled to be completed by the end of the day shift on Sunday.

One of the journeymen millwrights was Glen Breeding, a team leader who I mentioned earlier as being one of the best millwrights working anywhere in the Rouge complex. Glen, who was of average height and weight, had transferred to Rouge Steel several years before I got there. And, even though he was always in fairly good condition, he ended up being susceptible to a heart attack.

I can remember quite clearly when I was younger and working with him in the Dearborn Stamping Plant that he was one of several guys who took turns bringing doughnuts in for their morning coffee. This was a daily ritual that continued while working in the Steel Division, until he returned from having the heart attack. Now he was substituting bagels for the doughnuts, which was OK, but still not really that healthy.

Glen was a rather quiet guy who kept a lot of things to himself. He would talk to you if you asked him about something, but he wasn't much for making regular conversation. The reason I'm mentioning this is because he was a very dedicated worker who always tried to do the best he could, and if he was paired up on a job with someone who didn't like to work, or who was half- assed lazy, Glen would work extra hard to get the amount of work completed that he set out to do for that day or night.

So, getting back to that night job, I remember coming back to our lineup room after finishing our job and having some of the guys ask me if I had heard about Glen. I said, "No, what are you talking about?" They said he was taken out of the plant in an ambulance, and that they thought he had another heart attack.

Needless to say, I along with everyone else was totally stunned. No one seemed to know for sure just exactly what might have happened. There was some talk that Glen was working harder than he should have been because he was paired up with some guy or guys who were not carrying their share of the load. But that was only speculation, and I can't say any more than that, except that it was in an area where it was quite hot and that the heat might have been a contributing factor.

The sad part was that Glen was unable to survive to tell us about what had happened. This was, without a doubt, one of the greatest trage-dies I experienced in my thirty-three years of working in the Rouge. I liked and respected Glen Breeding very much and was upset for days and weeks afterward, as I'm sure quite a few other guys were as well.

I started keeping a diary ever since our kids were old enough to par-ticipate in sports. I became so wrapped up in it that I started writing about everything that was happening in our hectic life at this time, including things at work. The following is what I wrote about Glen after his tragic death:

Friday, August 9, '96 – This past Tuesday morning at Rouge Steel was one of the saddest days at work for my fellow workers and myself, as one of our senior millwright leaders, Glen Breeding, died of a heart attack.

Glen had a history of heart trouble – he had surgery about eight or ten years ago, but was doing quite well. Glen was a very smart and dedicated worker. If he had a weakness, it was that he tried to do too much work himself sometimes, instead of delegating others to do it. And, this might very well have been a contributing factor to his death.

When I came back from my weeklong vacation Monday night for Tuesday, Glen was sitting in our coffee shop working on a crossword puzzle, as he so often did. The #2 furnace in the Hot Mill was down the next two weeks for repairs and Glen, who normally worked days, was in on midnights for the start of a double shift.

I personally wondered why he would do this on such a hot, muggy day when the temperature was hovering around 90 degrees outside. Perhaps it was because he had a new job on days. Glen had just taken over the clerk's job from his old buddy, Dick "Killer" Kowalski, who was recently elected vice-president of our maintenance and construction unit.

Glen had been subbing for Killer for quite a while lately, and therefore, it was a smooth transfer for him to step in and take his place. The guys had said Glen was talking about purchasing a new house, so perhaps that was one of the reasons he was in on this miserably hot night.

There was also talk that he got shafted that night because his assigned partners were an apprentice, who wasn't exactly Mr. Gung Ho, and one of our female journeyman millwrights who had just graduated sometime in the last year and a half.

They ended up having some problems on their job, and Glen, as usual, took it onto his self to get the job done. Upon returning to the shop after their job was completed, he decided to take a shower to clean up and cool off.

While doing this he started to get some chest pain and so after dressing he went back to our shop area and walked up the stairs to the next level where the offices were located to ask the boss to take him to our Central Medical building. This was around 4am.

We couldn't understand why he did this, because as a leader, he always had a radio with him and could have easily called our boss, Less Harris, on that.

As they got in a van and started for Central Medical, they noticed that they had a visitor in the back of the van. Harry Walker, another millwright leader from days, who was also working a double, was lying down taking a nap during his lunch break.

Harry made the trip with them and stayed by Glens side until they took him away to Oakwood Hospital, where he was pronounced dead.

Later that same morning, around 7am, Less came back in our coffee shop to see us before we went home. We could easily see that he was visibly upset. He kept saying, "He didn't make it, he didn't make it."

I looked at Ernie Leonard, our millwright leader, and he looked at me as if to say, 'What the hell is he talking about?' He then said, "Glen Breeding, he had a heart attack and was taken to Oakland where he died early this morning."

We were all speechless and in a state of shock. We just sat there shaking our heads and trying to understand how something like this could possibly happen, which of course, you can't do, because it can happen to anyone at any time.

The millwrights in J-9 were very upset because none of the day-shift bosses went to the funeral. The only one to go was our boss, Less Harris, who was the boss at the time Glen was stricken.

They went to the visitation, but still could have sent someone to the funeral."

All the things that Glen had done to save their asses throughout the years, and what kind of appreciation do they show? Not enough, that's how we all felt. Not enough. And, that's the last thing that I wrote in my journal about that sad experience.

Another tragedy in the steel division involved my buddy, Tom Czarnomski, who transferred from Ford to Rouge Steel on the same day I did in 1990.

A few years or so after this, Tom had a heart attack that he survived and even managed to come back to work for a couple years or so before having another heart attack.

I believe he was out boating with his family, which he really enjoyed doing. His family was very important to him, and so he always tried to set time aside for them. This time, however, Tom was unable to pull through this fatal blow to his health.

Once again, we were all extremely shocked and saddened. I talked with his family at the funeral home and told them about how Tom and I used to discuss all of the things that were going on in our lives at the time, and how much he enjoyed watching his boys participate in sports.

I enjoyed our conversation very much, and I think they did also. Tom's one son, Mike, whom he talked about quite often, found some of the stories his dad and I talked about quite interesting. So, as I headed home that evening, I felt good that I was able to let them know that their dad and husband was a good caring man who loved his family very much, which I'm sure they knew anyhow.

Tom and I were also involved, along with another millwright, Rich Malinowski, in an interesting stock purchase.

One day while working together, we were talking about this company called Optical Imaging Systems (OIS) that was making flat screens for the U.S. government. They were receiving money grants from the government to help develop these screens and the business had been doing exceedingly well in the short period of time since it started up.

We all decided to purchase some of the stock because it was at a very reasonable price, something like $3.50 a share. Actually, some guys had purchased the stock a few months or so earlier for around $1.50 to $2.00 a share.

We all bought about the same amount of shares, somewhere around 1,500 to 3,000 shares. Everything was really looking up. In fact, it was doing so well that they purchased some property only a few miles from where we were living in Plymouth. I believe it was in the area of Beck and 5 or 6 Mile

Road. They then built an awesome state-of-the-art building that was supposedly the one big thing they needed to help the company take off, what with all the government grants. The stock eventually rose to around $11 or $12 a share. The three of us thought that there would be no question that it would continue to grow and probably reach close to $20 a share or more.

There was never any thought of selling any of the penny stock, as such stock is often called, even though we had more than tripled our money, which turned out to be a big mistake.

So, when the stock started to slide a little, we didn't think anything of it. We thought that was just the way stocks perform – up and down. When the stock slid back down to about $7.00 a share, I thought that would be a good time to buy some more because all of the write ups in the paper about OIS were very favorable. I thought there would be no doubt that it would turn around and climb back up towards our goal of $20.00 a share.

Big mistake!! It seemed that there was one set back after another. A fire or two, and a series of bad management decisions at this new location caused the stock to continue to plummet downward.

OIS eventually went out of business, and I learned the hard way that it is usually a good idea to sell off some of your stock after it had doubled or tripled to at least get your money out of it. Tough lesson learned.

CHAPTER 15

The New Dude Crew

By this time things were starting to change quite a bit at Rouge Steel. Many of the old guard had transferred back to Ford and retired. This in turn caused the largest influx of new blood at this huge complex in the twenty–plus years that I had been there.

Rouge Steel especially had hired quite a few apprentices in the spring of 1992, which turned the higher seniority tradesmen, such as myself, into teachers. I actually liked this, as long as the people I was working with were willing to listen and learn and weren't afraid to get their hands dirty.

One of the best ways to learn is through on-the-job training. Our bosses wanted these kids to get in there and get their hands dirty and learn the jobs, they did not want them standing around watching the journeyman do all the work.

Two of the better young guns were the sons of buddies of mine. One was Eric Rosenau, the son of Rosey, who was definitely following in his dad's footsteps as an excellent millwright. The other apprentice who was doing a fine job was another youngster by the name of Eric. He was the son of Drexel Ray, a millwright who I had worked with in the DSP for years before we both transferred to Rouge Steel.

Eric Ray was on a course to become a millwright boss, just like his dad. Anyhow, some of these new green horns became known as the "Dude

Crew." It was dude this and dude that, but putting all of that aside, for the most part they were good and willing workers, who, by the way, were not all men either.

We had three young ladies in our area who were millwrights. Kathie was one who was actually in her thirties and had some previous experience of working with tools. She eventually married one of our good young millwright journeymen by the name of Danny. They ended up buying a nice piece of property with a fix-it-up cabin on it somewhere around Sault Ste. Marie near the St. Mary's River. They loved it so very much that they were driving up there nearly every chance they could get. And who could blame them?

Julie, the daughter of one of our older millwrights, and Susie were the other two millwright apprentices. They all did a good enough job so as not to be singled out by anyone. Oh, there were a few complaints every once in a while, but no more than for anyone else. You might be wondering how these women fit into a male-dominated environment, so I thought I would tell this little short story.

One particular day, a high seniority journeyman millwright, who was in charge of our tool crib at the time, and who seemed to think that he was one step above the rest of us, came into our coffee shop and proceeded to pick out a seat close to where Julie was sitting. She was maybe twenty-one years old at the time. Several other millwrights were gathered at the end of the table and everyone was talking.

This guy proceeded to blend into the conversation, but he had to spice it up real nice with a bunch of F and MF bombs, way more than what should have been necessary. Actually, they weren't really necessary. He was just telling a story, and that's the way it continued to go. For whatever reason, he was making a bad attempt to be cool around Julie. Acting like Mr. Nice Guy while getting away with using all this foul language around her.

Today, with all the things that have been going on in the media with women filing one complaint after another in regard to sexual harassment, it's hard to believe that this would be tolerated.

The men, when talking amongst themselves, didn't hold back their language when she was in the room, but when she was directly involved in a conversation, as in this one, they had a little more respect for her. Oh, they might slip up every now and then, but not on purpose the way he was doing. I know she pretended not to let it bother her, but I'm sure that after a while, she became tired of hearing his bull crap.

So, things were definitely beginning to change at Rouge Steel. New and younger blood was coming in, and they were slowly starting to assert themselves, which was certainly needed.

The reason I am saying this is because many of the tools that we worked with, for the most part, were larger and heavier than those in any of the Ford production plants, just because of the nature of the work for producing steel.

For example, some of the jobs in the Hot Mill required a large over-head crane, rated at 50-100 tons, to pick up a large air impact and socket that required two millwrights to operate. This was done so that they could loosen huge hex nuts that were tightened down on very large threaded rods that held many of these machines and rollers together.

Complicating matters and making conditions even more difficult was the fact that it was usually quite hot up there on top of those machines, and, as though that wasn't enough, there was oil and grease everywhere. This meant that we had to be extremely careful and watch every step we took, while working on these types of jobs because it was easy too easy to throw one's back out while sliding around up there. Believe me it wasn't fun.

Once millwrights reach fifty, their bodies start to breakdown, especially after working long hours under conditions such as these. Most of them around this age have probably had at least one or two shoulder surgeries, along with countless back issues. And I of course, was no exception.

Without a doubt, an aging maintenance work force in the Steel Division was a big problem. So, because of this, we were only too happy to see the first group of apprentices that came through the program finally start to graduate and become full-fledged journeymen.

They were anxious to show that they could handle all of the many jobs in the different plant locations that our J-9 crews were responsible for and we were more than happy to see them feel this way.

The Rouge is an extremely huge complex, as I stated before, and on the Steel Division side there was the Hot Strip, which was our number one customer. We did nearly all of its dirty, nasty, maintenance work that no one there wanted to do. However, we didn't get the high incentive that those workers got, and that really upset us big time to say the least.

This, of course, is why they had J-9 over there all the time doing breakdowns and preventive maintenance. We were making significantly less incentive than their millwrights, and so, rather than hire more expensive millwrights to help do these jobs, they farmed them out to us at J-9.

One of the other buildings that we did a lot of work for was the Blast Furnace. They only had a few millwrights around this area during the last five or six years that I worked at Rouge Steel – just a small skeleton crew – and once again, whenever a big-time problem developed, we were the ones sent over there to do the work. In fact, during those last few years, we were over there nearly every other weekend doing regular repairs, fixing break-downs, and doing other general work that needed to be done by millwrights and riggers.

Without a doubt, most all of the buildings we worked in were very dangerous, but I think that the Blast Furnace was possibly the one building we all knew that we had to be extra careful around. This was mainly due to its age and all of its many built in dangers, such as extremely high air pressure combined with the obvious high heat areas. Nearly everywhere we walked around the outside perimeter of these old furnaces was highly hazardous. I would hate to see what would happen if a person got hit by a blast of highly pressurized air. Just the tiniest fracture in one of those lines could cut through a person like a sharp knife going through butter. Not good!!

One night, a hatch cover from on top of one of the Blast Furnaces blew off due to excessive interior pressure. It was found lying on the ground over

200 feet from where it came off. Fortunately, no one was working around this area when this accident happened. Another bullet dodged!

So, you can easily understand why we weren't overly excited about working on these jobs, especially since a lot of the work was done at night, which made it even more dangerous. Although we had numerous lights set up around the work area, it all came down to the fact that we just never knew when something was going to blow up or explode, and believe me, this was on everyone's mind. We tried to not let it bother us, but subconsciously, I'm sure that it did. Even though I have been retired since 1998, I still have nightmares about some of those dangerous midnight jobs.

The molten steel from the Blast Furnace was moved via huge ladles to the relatively new Concast building, where it was then made into 8-inch-thick x 4 or 5-foot-wide x 20-foot-long or longer slabs. These slabs where then transported by huge haulers, such as the Kress Slab Carrier, to the Hot Strip. Once there, they would get loaded onto large rollers by an overhead crane and run through more furnaces. This would then be followed by a series of even larger rolls, where each slab was slowly flattened out while still hot and flexible and gradually brought down to a thickness of around 1/16 to 3/16 of an inch.

As the steel started to become flat, it was cooled down with water sprinklers that were located throughout the process. By this time, it would be strung out down the line on smaller faster rollers and led into a coiler where it could be coiled to the necessary length. It would then be banded up and made ready to be hauled over to the Cold Mill, where it would be annealed and then finally sent over to the galvanizing building if required.

The Basic Oxygen Furnace (BOF) was another building that supplied molten steel to the Concast to be made into these huge slabs. Every so often, this building would have a problem that required additional help, so because of this we would be able to get some extra OT which was usually welcomed.

I found the BOF to be fairly similar to the Electric Arc in that it was extremely hot, noisy, and dangerous. One obvious difference was that it was also known for a residue from the steel making process that floated around in the air like snowflakes and could be found just about anywhere you looked.

Some people referred to this fallout residue as graphite flakes, while others called it kish. No matter what it was called, it was a pain in the butt because it got all over everything. I can remember as an apprentice getting these silver flakes all over my street cloths while standing in line to punch out. Not good!

The Cold Mill, which was located right next to our J-9 area in the old Rolling Mill, was also one of our main customers. In fact, the last year that I was there, which was 1998, we were working more and more OT in that building. Most of this work involved changing work rolls, which were the larger rolls that the steel rolled on during various treatment stages. These stages preceded the final annealing process, where the now coiled steel rolls were set in large annealing ovens and baked for a certain amount of time.

Once this annealing process was completed, the coiled steel was shipped across Miller Road to the Galvanizing Plant, which was better known as Double Eagle, because of its location near the Double Eagle pass, a small crossroad in that area.

Double Eagle galvanizing was, without a doubt, a huge money maker for Rouge Steel. Any time there was down time in that plant, we would have large crews over there to make the necessary repairs or do preventive maintenance and then get out as quickly as possible so they could start their lines running once again.

Most of the time that I was at Rouge Steel, J-9 typically kept one millwright leader over there, Rich Malinowski, and one or two other millwrights. They stayed in a sixty-foot trailer that we had stationed there as a sort of headquarters and meeting place for when the rest of our crew was summoned to help out.

Rich and his two-man crew did whatever daily jobs they could do while the lines were running. He would usually meet with their bosses every morning for a few minutes and they would discuss what the game plan would be for that day.

I know from firsthand experience that they always had something going on that needed the millwright's attention. And, if it was a job that required a welder, Rich would call the J-9 maintenance shop and have them send him one. My buddy Tom Czarnomski was one of the other millwrights stationed there, along with another rather funny guy by the name of Raul Annis. Anyhow, this one summer Raul had to take an extended medical leave and, because I had more seniority than a few other guys and was able to get along with Rich, who some of the other guys were not able to, I was asked to go over there. I didn't have to, but I thought at the time it would be a good change of pace, plus a chance to get to know that building better, which I wanted to do. Also, I liked the idea of working with Tom again.

So now, with me over there, we had an all-Polish connection: Malinowski, Czarnomski, and Moore (my mom's maiden name was Szymoniak). We would often joke around with a lot of old Polish phrases and the way our parents or grandparents used them.

I think I ended up working at Double Eagle for several months before checking back in at J-9, where I eventually was able to climb aboard the midnight shift. However, before going on about that, I just wanted to say that the reason I have mentioned something about all of these buildings is to let you have an idea of what an adventure it was working in this giant Rouge Complex, which encompasses over 2,000 square acres.

Most of the higher seniority millwrights that worked at the Rouge around the same time span that I did, and those who preceded me, nearly all had the valuable experience of working at many of these plants throughout the complex, as opposed to spending a whole career in just one or two buildings.

This is why as apprentices we moved around so often, to gain that valuable experience in many different buildings, which helped us become extremely, well rounded, skilled tradesmen.

To this day, I still insist that the skilled tradesmen in the Rouge Complex, especially the millwrights and welders, are some of the most versatile and experienced tradesmen found anywhere in the world.

I know that I had a wonderful opportunity to learn a lot from every building I worked in. And, for someone such as myself, who came from more of a sports-oriented background, it was a godsend. This is one of the reasons why I decided to write this book – to give everyone else a little peak into what it was like working in this world-famous complex for Ford Motor Company and Rouge Steel for thirty-three years. It was truly amazing.

CHAPTER 16

J-9 Related Stories

After returning to the J-9 shop area just before going on midnights, I spent a couple of months working with the tinsmiths on some special projects that also required some millwright work.

One of the "tinnies" welders was a guy who was better known as Chicken, and was one of the most notorious welders in the Rouge Complex.

Skilled tradesmen, millwrights and welders in particular, were, and probably still are, known for their hard drinking and rather wild lifestyle.

In his younger days, and while I was still an apprentice in the Power House, Chicken was in his prime as a big boozer. It seemed like every time I had to work with him, he wanted me to talk. He didn't really care what it was about, but he had to have steady conversation.

He never used to give a damn about anything because his wife had plenty of money, so consequently, he was absent a lot. We all thought that if he had kept this pace up, he wouldn't be around too much longer. And it was really a shame because "Chicken" was an excellent welder and a good worker when he was on the job. As an apprentice I remember getting some good tips from him as to how to set certain jobs up to make it easier for him to weld.

After meeting him again in the tin shop, I learned that he had done a great job of turning his life around and straightening things out. Now he was coming in to work on time and seldom missed a day. I definitely felt good for him. He looked much better and must have felt better, too, because he was always very friendly and in a pretty good mood. Good job man!

While I'm on the subject, I must say that I had never actually seen anyone doing hard drugs at work, like shooting up heroin or sniffing cocaine, but that doesn't mean it did not happen.

Pot, of course, was another story, it was the most commonly used street drug, so it was no big deal. I knew a small group of guys who went out for lunch nearly every day to a certain party store, Jim's Market, that also sold subs and sandwiches. They would get some beer, along with something to eat, and then hang out in the parking lot, smoking pot and drinking beer with an occasional bottle of liquor being passed around.

Most of us knew who these guys were, so if any one of them happened to be working in our crew, we would be a little more careful working around them. Occasionally, if someone came back a little too high while we were out in the field away from the shop area, they could lie down in the back of one of the pickups or vans that we used for transportation to and from the job site. We didn't want any of them working around us when they were like that and, fortunately, it didn't happen too often. This generally worked OK, unless one of the bosses happened to catch someone doing this, and then the guy would get docked an hour or so, or sent home if he was really messed up. There were a number of guys who could not even drive because they had their license suspended, so if they ended up getting sent home early, they would have to hang out around our coffee shop until the end of the shift until someone came to give them a ride home. Every so often, we would hear of something goofy happening on a job after lunch. Something such as structural iron being hung the wrong way or in the wrong spot. Once we found out that it was one of these guys working the job, we understood what caused the problem.

Most of the time however, the bosses knew better than to put too many of these guys together on the same job. They would usually split them up so that they would be working with other crews. Because of all the exposure, these guys were a little more careful about going out for a toke if they had a job working inside the shop area.

I'm not making excuses for this type of behavior, but it was very stressful and tough working all of that OT day after day and under all of those hazardous conditions that we were constantly being asked to work around. We knew guys were struggling to get a good night's sleep at home, which meant that towards the end of the work week they would be a little more tired and worn out and more susceptible to making mistakes and possibly getting injured or injuring someone else. So, because of this, we were always watching out for and trying to help someone who had been putting in too many hours in the last few weeks. It was like a family, and we didn't want to see anyone get injured. We had to take care of each other because it could get pretty brutal and I'm damn proud to say that I was a survivor from all of those hectic and challenging days.

Also, so as not to be a hypocrite, I must say that I have taken a swig or two of brandy from a bottle that was passed around our locker room, and also in our lineup room. However, that was at Christmas time, and on the last day of work before Christmas Eve.

This was the day we had our big Christmas party, and it wasn't uncommon for this to happen each year. As a matter of fact, I would usually bring in a quart-size bottle of Leroux Jezynowka, a great tasting Polish blackberry brandy for everyone to try. Harry Walker, one of our good senior millwright leaders, had a locker across from mine, and he couldn't say enough good things about it. More than likely, if I know Harry, he said it so he could get another swig, which he usually did. Anyhow, we were not doing anything different for that time of year than anyone else. Nearly every business has some sort of Christmas party.

So even though pot wasn't anything to get too excited about, it was one of many things that was going on in and around the Frame Plant around 1990 that had everyone talking. There was, and perhaps still is, a large parking lot across from the Frame Plant, and outsiders could easily walk into the complex from there, because there were hardly ever any security guards at that gate, which was always wide open. To me, this was just asking for trouble, and trouble is what they got.

There were other gates that they could occasionally sneak through, but this was the easiest one. In the spring of 1990, a woman and her baby were seen sitting inside the complex begging for money for the homeless. Instead of just quietly asking her to leave, security ended up surrounding her with a bunch of their cars and made a big scene over it. I am not sure if the Dearborn police were ever called in. If they were, one would think that they would have suggested better security in that area.

This just turned out to be a small incident compared to all of the prostitutes, dope dealers, and bums – just about anything and everything that was over there and in that parking lot that everyone was talking about. Drug deals were taking place on a daily basis. Now that I think about it, I wouldn't be surprised, if someone wasn't getting their palms greased to look the other way.

I once saw a couple of guys come out of the Frame Plant and throw a large roll of something over that parking lot fence to some guys on the other side. There was a pedestrian door nearby, so it was easy for them to do this and then disappear without being seen. The only thing I cannot remember about that is what time of the day it was, except that it was near a shift change, because I was in my car heading home as this little caper was taking place.

Since the time when all of that was taking place, Rouge steel has been sold a couple of times. In February of 2004, the Russian Company Severstall Steel held the reigns until 2014 when AK Steel took over the owner-ship and now everything has completely changed. Security cameras have been placed all over the place making it much more difficult to leave the plant before the end of the shift. I know that has to make a lot of people happy. Not!

I was made aware of many of these changes that first started to be implemented by Severstall Steel from my old millwright buddy Fred Goroni. He called just before the first of the year in 2006 after seeing a picture of myself and my two daughters on the front page of the Detroit Free Press under the headline "Driven Away - How The Auto Industry Lost A Generation".

The article, which was written by Joe Guy Collier and Kortney Stringer, talks about how and why the new generation of young workers, such as my daughters, are more willing to take jobs with companies other than the Big Three, rather than follow in the footsteps of their relatives who worked in the auto industry.

Reprinted with permission of Detroit Free Press

As a result of reading that compelling article, I wrote this following poem, A Changing Auto World.

A Changing Auto World

The auto industry is no longer a family tradition. Sadly, it's become an altogether different rendition.

The new generation can plainly see the hand writing on the wall and is now hesitant to enter into an industry that is so unsteady and looking too much like a once proud empire that is about ready to fall.

Yes, the men and women of the Big Three are still doing the very best that they can, but now are being asked to take huge benefits and wage cuts while still being expected to bust their butts.

They still want to do a good job of making the best cars in the world, but without leaders with vision and futuristic ideas and plans, they will play second fiddle to countries that were once thought by our auto executives to be insignificant and way too little.

That's right! We brought the Asians and Europeans into our plants and showed them our technology and now they have improved upon it and have us singing a different song and wondering, what could possibly have gone wrong?

We need more leaders such as William Clay Ford Jr. who saved the Dearborn Rouge Ford Complex from certain death by giving it a shot of fresh air and a new breath.

His push towards hybrid cars and especially the use of ethanol as an alternative fuel, could turn out to be like a diamond in the rough – a real jewel.

Why not use one of our greatest assets – our hard-working farmers and their fertile land to help bail us out of this hole we've dug for ourselves and make us stand tall and be proud once again, man?

We can do it. It won't be easy, but by sticking together and working hard, we will succeed once again and be proud to show off our UAW card!

Fred is retired and has moved from living in Kentucky for a few years to taking up residence once again in the Southern Michigan area. He is able to keep up with what is going on in the Rouge through relatives and friends that might still be working there. If it's something that he thinks I might be interested in he will give me a call with the latest update.

Fred has always been a good story teller and this is a story he relayed to me about the time he had a pass to drive into the plant. This was usually given out only by the medical department if they felt the employee had not fully recovered from some type of injury he had and would aggravate it by making the long walk into the plant from the parking lot. This could be as much as 1/8 of a mile or more from our shop.

Fred explained that this one particular day he was late into the second half of a double shift and wasn't feeling too well. Since things were pretty quiet and there wasn't too much going on, and since he didn't live too far away from the plant, he decided to leave for home early.

He let the guys he was working with know what he was planning to do, so that they could cover for him if something came up at the last minute. Sure enough, shortly after getting home, the phone rings, and it's one of the guys saying the boss was looking for him.

Fred said that he drove back into the plant, called the boss from the millwright shop on the in–plant phone, updated him with what they had been doing, and then jumped into his car and went back home. Amazing!

Fred and I often talked about how dangerous the Steel Division was, which led to another story about a day when he and a fellow millwright by the name of Terry Szarbo were on a job when a rigger was operating an overhead crane with a remote-control box. The guy happened to run the cable block too far up on the crane, causing the 1-Inch diameter cable to break loose from the block and come down whipping around like a snake as it hit the floor. As this happened, the loose ends of the cable caught Fred, who as I said before, is around 6 foot 2 inches tall and 215 pounds, around the knees. It knocked him down and then it hit Terry's arm so hard it swelled up so much that he had to spend a day or two in the hospital.

Fred said that a taxi brought him back to the plant from the hospital after being thoroughly checked out. And, believe it or not, after going through all of this, his boss asked him to stay over and work a double shift. The man just came back from the hospital and here they were asking him to work over-time after he was so close to being severely injured. It was amazing, but what made it even more amazing was the fact that he actually agreed to do it.

I guess that's why the bosses often let the guys get away with so much, because it was difficult to get them to stay and work on certain jobs that were either extremely nasty or very dangerous, or worse yet, a combination of the two.

Another story Fred mentioned was about our friend, Henry Horn, who was injured once again while working around a crane. This time however, the cable block hit Henry's shoulder, causing him to miss several weeks of work.

It's no wonder he finally got out of the field and into a union job. I do not blame him one bit for not wanting to come back in coveralls. This was at least the third time that he had been injured quite badly, and that was three times too many.

Having seen and also heard of so many guys getting injured while on the job, I must give thanks that I was so very fortunate to be able to walk away from some potentially devastating injuries. Oh! I had my back and shoulder problems, almost cut my finger off, and injured my foot once or twice but hey, that was just life working in the famous Rouge Complex for Ford and Rouge Steel for thirty-three years.

Without a doubt, there was a lot of money to be made at Rouge Steel during the 1990's, especially in a lucrative building such as the Cold Mill, which was located next door to our J-9 area.

Rumor had it that a millwright by the name of Bobby was knocking down around $125,000 to $140,000 a year while working as many as five doubles a week or more on the midnight shift. I worked a lot of OT at J-9, where I was probably around number three or four in hours worked for the three years I was on midnights. This was out of a total of around forty-five or so millwrights, and I wasn't even close to those figures. I usually worked two or three doubles a week, if offered, and only a few times a year would I work as many as four. So what Bobby was doing over there was absolutely amazing, and all I can say in regard to that is "Best of luck with the home life!"

Sometime around 11:30 pm, August 1, 1995, our union and the company (Rouge Steel) agreed to a new five-year contract just before the current one was to expire at midnight.

We received a one-time six percent increase in base pay, plus our cost of living was rolled into our base pay. We also collected a $1,000 signing bonus (big deal, we would rather have had a better raise.) There would also be bonuses for the next four years, $500 minimum plus a percentage of the profits. The total of the two would not be over $1,000.

Also, we were awarded a stock buying program that was set up earlier in the year and counted as part of our new contract. This program was tied in with the Tax Efficient Savings Plan for Hourly Employees (TESPHE.)

I had fifteen percent, later it became eighteen percent, of the gross figure taken out of my check each week, and the company matched it.

If the contract would have been similar to the three years that they received at Ford's we would have been satisfied. Five years, however, was just too long to go with nothing better than what we received. And, because of this, we would be falling even further behind the pay scale for the workers at Fords and that definitely had a lot of people complaining.

The word was out that Rouge Steel wanted to keep our pay scale in line with the other steel companies, which is fine, but we had put Rouge Steel at the head of the list of steel companies and we thought our pay level should have reflected this.

The Rouge Steel workers had not had a significant pay raise in over ten years. In fact, they took huge pay deductions back in the early to mid-80's when steel companies from all over were in big trouble.

This was back when Ford Motor Company still owned the Steel Division, but was doing very little to help make it successful.

It was more of a headache to them than anything else, so they started looking to get rid of it. When I was an apprentice in the old Iron Foundry and the BOF, which was around 1973-75, the old millwrights were pulling in huge bucks because of all the incentive money they received on their check each week. A good incentive week in the BOF would add an extra $300-$350 or more to a millwright's take-home pay.

No wonder the competition to get into the Steel Division was so keen back in the '60's and '70's. No wonder most of the millwrights and welders over there had a couple of brand-new cars and a twenty-four-foot boat sitting in front of their garage and a beautiful vacation home up north. No wonder Ford sold the Steel Division when they did. Actually, it was a wonder that they did not sell it sooner.

Carl Valdisari, a veteran Steelman, who knew the ins and outs of steel making as well as anyone, eventually bought the division in the fall of 1989 and did an excellent job of turning it around and making it profitable.

But getting back to the five-year contract, the only way we could make any big money anymore was by working considerable amounts of OT. Our hourly pay, and especially our incentive, at J-9 was so pitiful that a forty-hour check per week just wasn't good enough.

Fortunately, there was plenty of OT being offered, but as soon as that slacked off, the guys would start bitching about how we got screwed again with our contract.

Sometime in March of 1996, our overtime did finally get cut back, and that meant one of our biggest project jobs, the annealing furnace bases that we had been working on for the last few months or so, had been put on hold. The company would end up letting them go until they were forced to repair them and then they would want to rush us through the job so that they could get it running again.

These jobs usually lasted two or three weeks, depending on how much damage there was to the sidewalls, floor pan, and underlying support beams, but if there was any kind of extensive damage, it could easily take over a month to finish up the work.

So, they decided to postpone these jobs, as I said, until they were forced to repair them, which meant that someone could possibly end up getting injured. Even before we started working on these annealing bases, we were doing structural iron repair work in the basement area of the Cold Mill. This was because of the seemingly endless presence of acid floating around in the air, which over a period of many years, had made its presence felt.

Rusted out beams and braces were easily seen throughout this area and had to be repaired or replaced, depending on the extent of the damage. Our welders hated these nasty jobs because of all the poisonous fumes that resulted from burning and welding around these ancient bases, especially in the warm weather months.

They would have to wear tight-fitting respirators around these jobs and, of course, this meant that they would be sweating a lot, and because of all of the acid in the air, their neck and face areas would start itching and burning. Not fun!

CHAPTER 17

A Return to Midnights at J-9

It was in the Spring of 1996 and I was definitely happy to be working midnights once again. I was healthy for the first time in quite a while and was looking forward to having the opportunity to work some OT and make some extra money.

It had been a year or so since J-9 had a midnight shift, and therefore, Dick Sapula, who was to be our millwright leader, Greg Thole another millwright, Sonny Wright our welder, and myself decided we would do a real good job for our boss, Less Harris, so that the management team on days would not want to shut this shift down – and it worked. They decided to keep the shift going as long as we continued to accomplish whatever it was that they had set up for us to do for that particular night or week.

It was good that everyone agreed to go all in on this. That way we were able to give them what they wanted most of the time and then some, which made our boss look good, and which in turn was good for all of us on this shift.

We worked together for several months until our good young welder, Sonny, was bumped onto days by a higher seniority welder by the name of Tool Time Tim McCann.

Actually, Sonny might have had to go on days because of some complications that developed concerning his Hodgkin's disease. He had been taking cobalt treatments for the last year or so, and quite often, would be too sick and weak after the treatment to come in to work.

We really missed Sonny because he was always willing to help us if we needed an extra pair of hands for something. He was also very good with a cutting torch in his hands. I worked with some very good welders before, but he was one of the best at making a nice clean cut. He could burn a hole in a piece of steel so well that it looked as though it was done with a drill. We were all pulling for him to get well again. Modern medicine can do fantastic things, so hopefully he made out all right.

I had met Tim McCann while I was working in the DSP, so I was familiar with him and knew that he was also a good worker. This new crew, however, was also to be short- lived because one of the millwright leaders on days, Ernie Leonard, decided he wanted to work nights, and so when the bumping period came, he bumped Dick back on to days.

Tool Time Tim's stay on midnights was also short, since a welder by the name of Terry Peipers bumped him. After this latest bump, the main core of our midnight shift for the next two years or so was pretty much set, with Ernie as the Millwright leader and myself and Greg Thole as the other two millwrights, along with Terry Peipers as our welder.

Ernie and I had something in common in that we were both raised in small, northeastern, Michigan towns. He came from Posen, a small, pre-dominately Polish community just north of Alpena, and I came from the even smaller village of Millersburg, which is maybe twenty miles north of Posen in Presque Isle County.

Eventually, an apprentice millwright and welder were added to our shift to help us keep up with all the work that was beginning to develop. There were a lot of things going on during these years. It seemed like as soon as we finished one big project, there was another one waiting for us. Every once in a while, we would even get a job where we could have a little fun.

One week, we were working over by the Electric Arc Furnace, cleaning up the yard about a year or so after it had closed down. There was a lot of scrap metal and equipment spread out all over this area that needed to be cut up before we could move it into large scrap gondolas. We also had to use Hi-Lo and cherry pickers (portable cranes) to move and reposition a lot of structural iron that was randomly lying around.

One particular night while we were in the middle of doing this work, we happened to see a couple of red foxes slinking around the yard. The next night, Ernie brought in a can of dog food. We opened it up and took it over to the job with us and sat it on top of some 24 to 30-inch scrap metal bails.

Within a half hour or so, a whole family of the critters were out there snooping around that can. They had been denning up in some of the loose cavities between the huge piles of bailed up scrap steel. We watched them every night for the rest of the week until we finished that job. First, one would come out, followed by another, and another. I believe there were about five or six in all.

The little ones didn't behave too differently than what eight-month-old puppies would. They darted in and out of the large back door opening of the Electric Arc, jumping and crawling around on some of the old machinery, simulating a game of tag or hide and seek.

Jobs like this did not come along too often, so we had to enjoy them when they did. Of course, one might get lucky and end up working with someone like Walt Colby, a millwright who often provided entertainment for those working with or around him.

One day, Walt went ballistic while changing shear blades in the Cold Mill. Shear blades are the large blades that shear the rolled out flat steel as it passes through different stations along the line.

He was having quite a bit of trouble getting a bolt to work loose from its hole, and he started to go bonkers, almost throwing his hammer at it. I guess that's why I always liked Walt, because I was kind of like that too. In fact, I'm sure anyone who has ever struggled with some sort of mechanical problem knows the feeling.

Walt, too often however, had to take things one step further. He was known to do some very unpredictable things, such as what he did one day after lunch outside the old Rolling Mill. He didn't feel like taking the steps up to the roof of the building where his crew was working. Instead, he hopped onto the large ball and hook attached to the large cherry picker that they were using, hung onto the cable with heavy leather face gloves, and had the rigger who was operating the picker extend him all the way up to the top of the roof, which was probably seventy feet or so. Amazing! But what was even more amazing was the fact that the operator actually did it. They both could have been fired, or at least received some disciplinary action, such as three days or more off from work for pulling a stunt like that.

In the old days, the millwrights could get away with doing something like that, but with all of OSHA's rules and regulations, this was now a no-no, especially going up that high. But this was the Rouge and crazier things have happened.

Another flake was a welder by the name of Steve Biro, who had a substance abuse problem, but was doing an excellent job of controlling it. I'm sure he had his ups and downs, but at least he wasn't giving up. He was constantly fighting the problem.

He was also known to do some rather wild and crazy things, and so I wasn't too surprised when, one day, I heard he rode his motorcycle into a car in the parking lot. I believe he told me that he somehow managed to go between two yellow bumper posts and then slammed into this car. The date was around May of 1996, and again, this was another stunt that could go under the heading of amazing.

We also had a young apprentice by the name of Dilworth who was a ring freak. I don't remember too much about him, except what I jotted down in one of my notebooks and that referred to the fact that when he first started working with us, he had four rings in his nose (two on each side), three on each eyelid, and even some by his navel and his pecs, or so he said.

One day, he came in the coffee shop, lineup room, and most of the visible ones were gone. I believe he finally became tired of getting hassled over them all the time and decided to start taking his job a little more seriously. Perhaps he realized that this environment was no place for all that crazy Dennis Rodman stuff.

One other character was this big old millwright who I only knew by the nickname of Moose, which was actually quite appropriate because he must have been around 6 foot 2 inches tall and 250 pounds or so, and was rather slow on his feet.

I once overheard a locker room conversation about how Moose liked to gamble, which caused him to get caught up in some of the high-stakes poker games that used to take place in the Rouge. Moose ended up losing several thousand dollars and then put up a $10,000-$15,000 house he owned in the city, probably Detroit, because quite a few guys owned rental houses there, and he proceeded to lose that too.

These poker games were not limited to just Rouge employees either. Guys off the street were also known to be involved in some of these games, which often went on around the clock. It wasn't uncommon to see some of these workers hanging out well after their shift was over and doing nothing but playing high-stakes poker for hour after hour.

Moose worked in one of the highest incentive buildings, lucky him, so he probably made up his losses in a few months with a heavy load of OT.

All I can say is that it is hard to feel sorry for someone like this because he will probably turn around and gamble it all away again.

Another guy known as "Radio" was into a lot of extra-curricular activity. He used to run a huge check pool all over the Rouge that would sometimes pay as much as $8,000. He even told me one time that it wasn't uncommon for him to have as much as $10,000 in his pocket at times. Perhaps he was one of Big Ed Martin's lieutenants.

My buddy Fred Goroni once told me about an old worker whose name was Art Eckles, better known as The Big Buck, because it seemed that all he ever talked about was money and more money.

Fred said that it seemed as though this guy was willing to work as many hours as he could to make all that money. (This sounds a lot like my former neighbor and good friend Jimmy Rosenau who is now working back at Ford's in the new truck plant and loving every minute of it.) I had the opportunity to talk with Jim recently at a book signing that I did at the Dearborn Centennial Library along with a couple of ex bosses, Bernie and Dick Gatza, who was from the Steel Division. He told me that it feels like heaven after working all those tough years in the grease and oil of the Hot Strip. Also, before leaving, he mentioned that his son, Eric, ended up taking a very nice buyout from Severstall Steel, and has found an exceptionally good job, if I remember correctly, out west.

I told Rosey that he deserved a great job like that and that I found out what an awesome plant it was when my wife Debbie and I went through the truck plant as part of the Greenfield Village Ford Rouge tour, which was amazing. I congratulated him again on his new job and wished him and his son Eric the best of luck.

In the mid '60's, The Big Buck was involved in an accident with a man lift. I guess he went flying out of the basket and hurt himself bad enough to be off work for over a year. When he returned, it was like nothing had happened. He went right back to working as much OT as before – money, money and more money.

According to Fred, The Big Buck was old (maybe forty or so) when Fred started as an eighteen-year-old apprentice. The fact that he was still working when Fred retired sometime around 2002 was unbelievable. The guy had to be around seventy-eight years old or so. As amazing as it may sound, I have heard about, and also seen, men that same age or even older do the same thing. I think they would be totally lost without the camaraderie of their workplace. It's rather sad, but that's their whole life.

CHAPTER 18

Slider Night and Changes at J-9

Sometime around late summer and fall of 1996, there were quite a few changes being made in the J-9 area of Rouge Steel, which made me glad I was working midnights.

One of our foremen, Jerry, "The Catman" Catalano, was made a general foreman, and he didn't waste any time setting things up the way he wanted them. Unfortunately, the way he went about doing this was pissing a lot of people off, including the other foremen who worked for him.

Around the middle of December, Al Kukan resigned as a boss and went back to working as a millwright. He was only on supervision for about a year, if that long, and they were making him work all kinds of OT and refused to give him any kind of raise. He was making less than a dollar an hour more than a non-salaried worker and all that OT just wasn't worth it.

He told me his wife was hassling him and calling him an idiot for working all the time. (What would we do without our wives?) Anyhow, his only recourse was to give that job up so he could get back to a more normal life and keep his family happy. Without a doubt, I would have to agree, that was a smart move.

Also, around this time, a couple of our good millwright leaders turned in their leadership titles, which carried an extra 45 cents per hour. However, there was always someone ready to step up to the next level. Bob Maciasz had been working in the planning department for several years, and we all knew it would only be a matter of time before he became a foreman and this was it.

Bob was a well-liked fellow around 5 foot 10 inches tall and 190 pounds, and was probably somewhere in his late thirties. He had enough experience to be able to handle any BS that The Catman might throw at him. In fact, one of his strongest suits was that he was very good at knowing how to tell people what they wanted to hear in order to appease them. Even with all of this going on, The Catman was riding high. Rouge Steel management must have been quite satisfied with the job he had been doing, because by 1998, my last year at the Rouge, he had been promoted to the job of super-intendent, which he took over from a long-time Rouge Steel boss, John Denton, who had recently retired.

Anyhow, that's what was happening on the day shift, but fortunately we were working the midnight shift and were more concerned with just trying to stay warm on any outside jobs at 2 o'clock in the morning on a cold winter night. Believe me, it wasn't easy, especially when tempers would flair up while we were rushing to get an assignment completed as soon as possible so that we could get back inside where it was warmer.

Here's a great example of what I'm talking about. One night while working midnights, we had a job that involved moving some large, long steel beams. I was operating the Broaderson cherry picker while Ernie Leonard and one of our young lady apprentices, Julie hooked the beams up.

Ernie, who could be a little gruff at times, was giving me what I thought were mixed signals and yelling at me at the same time, which started to get on my nerves. The problem was that Ernie, who it seemed was always in a big ass hurry, wanted me to speed it up a little, and I was trying to be a bit more careful, because it was a very large load that could easily swing away and hurt someone.

Julie could see that I was starting to get pissed off at Ernie, so she said something to him and that just added fuel to the fire. At this point, I cannot remember exactly what happened. I believe that I either let the load down or left it hanging (it wasn't up too high at that point, only a few feet or so) and started to get out of the Broaderson.

Ernie saw this and figured he better come up with something very quick, so he said something like, "You better get back on that picker," and I then yelled back something about him giving me better signals or he could get in there and operate it himself.

I guess that's all it took, because after that everything went quite smoothly and we were able to finish the job and get back to our coffee shop without anyone getting hurt.

Ernie and I got along alright for the most part because I knew how he was and didn't let it bother me too much. But sometimes after a long hard week of work, tempers would flare and there would be occasional confrontations such as this, but they didn't last long because we understood each other enough to know it was just job-related BS that could get on anyone's nerves.

Most of the time, it was outdoors in the middle of a cold December or January night when things like that happened. Working outside at 3 am during those months was never fun for anyone.

The last couple of years on midnights, nearly every Thursday that we did not have a major down time to deal with, we would send someone out at lunchtime to a White Castle for what they called Sliders. These little burgers were called sliders because they were so small and greasy that they would slide down your gullet quite effortlessly. Sliders were only about 1/8 of an inch thick or so, and some guys would ask for anywhere from seven to ten of those bad boys. Making matters even worse, they would order some jalapeno peppers to have with them.

Needless to say, it wasn't exactly fun having to work with any of these guys after they ate a meal like this. I always hedged on getting any sliders, but one night I let the guys talk me into it and so I ordered a few.

I ate them along with some of the jalapenos, and they ended up making me sick as a dog. So sick in fact, that I was unable to make my next shift. I know your probably thinking what a wimp I am, but it just shows how nasty those bad boys really were. Also, if I remember correctly, our boss Less had a few that night and said something about them making him feel pretty miserable as well.

My problem was that I seldom ate any red meat, and so my body was just reacting to all of that greasy fat. So, after that interesting experience, I would order a fish sandwich every once in a while, but I never ordered another one of those nasty sliders.

There were a lot of things happening my last few years at Rouge Steel, and most of them were not good.

Sometime in 1995, one of our millwright leaders, Rich Malinowski, who basically ran the Double Eagle galvanizing area for J-9, just missed being seriously injured when he caught a glancing blow to the head when a cable broke that was helping support a load he was lifting.

He was immediately taken to Oakwood Hospital, where they thoroughly checked him out and took a set of x-rays. The following day, he had to return for a CT-scan because of something they found in the first set of tests.

Fortunately, everything worked out alright for Rich, and he was able to resume his regular work after a week or so, but probably not before he took some good-natured kidding about what they might have found when they looked in his brain – a Polish vacuum. Just kidding, I'm Polish too.

In March of 1996, another one of our millwrights at J-9, Greg Burt, was working in the Hot Mill over the weekend and had his hand partially crushed, resulting in a couple of broken fingers.

Greg's crew was using an overhead crane operator to help out with their job when the operator made a move with the crane without being given a signal from any of the crew, which is a big no-no. Greg was not expecting the crane to move and consequently was injured because of this guy's carelessness.

Too often, the crane operators in that building would not do as they were directed. They would get in too big of a hurry and did not always work safely. A lot of this was because they had been drinking. Quite often they would run out to the bar at night, have a few drinks before it closed up and then come back all jacked up with an attitude. Their bosses knew these guys were doing this, but they continued to let them get away with it. Once again, amazing!

Another depressing thing that happened during this time was when one of our electricians was electrocuted while working on top of an overhead crane because he had not shut the main power source off. He then made the fatal mistake of touching something hot, which caused him to get fried.

Sometimes skilled tradesmen were so confident in what they were doing, that they would take short cuts to get the job completed a little quicker. The problem with that theory is that these short cuts didn't always work out the way they had envisioned, and when that happened and things went wrong, there was often a very huge price to pay.

Early in 1998, I started having quite a bit of trouble with my back once again. We were doing more and more jobs in the Cold Mill, specifically changing the shear blades that cut the steel as it came down the line.

This meant that we were constantly working around slippery machined surfaces and no matter how careful we were, we could still easily hurt ourselves because there was no way of avoiding these oily surfaces. All we could do was be careful, and anyone who has ever worked in these types of conditions, knows how easy it is to throw a back out while working in such an environment.

I can't remember exactly how it happened, but I ended up having to be placed on restrictions because of a bulging herniated disc in my back. I knew it would not be too long before I would have to go on days because of this, and I was right. Jerry "Catman" Catalano, who was now the day-shift superintendent, said I would be going on days and working in the tool crib with Billy Johnson, another millwright with back problems, and the boss would be Rich Cook. Rich was a very bright man who had been demoted from superintendent to foreman, mostly because of drinking problems and a penchant for voicing his opinion a little too forcefully when he knew he was right about something.

Rich was a good boss, and as long as someone was doing a good job, he wouldn't mess with them. This was unlike some of the other bosses who were always trying to one-up the other guy in an effort to make themselves look good.

This was also to be the start of my least productive year at Rouge Steel. I was limited to only certain types of jobs and, therefore, wasn't able to work much OT. Often times when they had a rough weekend lined up and they could not get enough high seniority men to come in and work, they would ask me to come in and more or less baby-sit some apprentices.

This worked alright as long as everything was going OK, but occasionally I would have to get involved and end up having to do something that I had no business doing. I did it in order to get the job done, but then I paid the price the next day with my back throbbing, which meant it would be a long time before I could work any OT again.

I was, without a doubt, getting bored working the day-in-day-out duties of the crib, which included handing out gloves and tools and setting up gang boxes for weekend work. Once the weekend was over, Johnson and I would have to go through all the gang boxes and clean everything up, and then re-arranges things so they would be ready for the next big job.

One of the few things I really liked about this job was when the guys would have some time to stop by the window and BS. That way I was able to keep up with everything that was going on out in the field and around the Rouge in general, and there was always a lot going on.

CHAPTER 19

Real Estate Squeeze and the Last Hoorah

In the spring of 1998, my wife and I started looking for property in northern Michigan where we could hopefully build a retirement house in a few years or so.

Since we were both from that area originally, we pretty much knew the boundaries of where we wanted to live, and so did my wife's sisters, who lived in the lovely, little, northeast lower peninsula town of Onaway, in Presque Isle County.

This definitely paid dividends for us, because they had recently looked at a very nice log house with seven acres situated on the beautiful, meandering Black River. They thought it was something we might be interested in, so they took some pictures of it and sent them to us.

We liked what we saw from the pictures, so we called the real estate agent and set up an appointment for the following weekend. The house was set back on the property off of the highway about 125 yards, surrounded by what was once a red pine plantation.

As we drove down the winding driveway, I could see there would be a lot of work in cleaning up all of the dead branches that were hanging so low to the ground, but it was also obvious that this was a beautiful location.

We ended up looking at that house several more times that summer. Finally, I decided to do a little math and ended up concluding that with my retirement check and my wife's income from working as a nurse at, what was at that time, Northern Michigan Hospital in Petoskey, we could make it work.

Deb called NMH to see if she could work out a deal to get hired, and once that was set, we made an offer on the house, which was eventually accepted. Then, we had to put our nice house in Plymouth on the market, because there was no way we could afford the property up north unless we sold this place. Eventually we did sell it, but not before getting a royal screw job.

The real estate agent we hired from the Plymouth area found an interested buyer and, of course, they both knew we had found this place up north, and so they conspired to play a little game with us. We had agreed to a set price for our house in Plymouth, which included the buyer putting $9,000 down.

It was getting close to our deadline to finalize the deal up north when the selling agent for our house in Plymouth said the buyer would not be able to install a large pole barn, as he wanted to do, in order to store and protect all of his antique cars. The reason for this was because of all the various township restrictions, and so he was going to back out of the deal, unless we agreed to drop the price of our house by approximately $9,000, which was the amount of his down payment.

I told my wife that I would love to tell the agent that we would not agree to do that, and that we would just keep this $9,000 deposit, but at the same time, the up north agent was also squeezing us, saying something about another couple being very interested in that property if we weren't going to follow through with our commitment to purchase it.

We knew that we were getting a bargain and did not want to chance losing it by giving up our downstate deal, so we decided to eat the $9,000 deposit and agree to their demand. It was still a very good deal for us, but it just shows how these shysters, I mean agents, work. So anyhow, we were finally all set to make our big move up north.

My last day at work, I was given a pass to take my tool box out of the plant. One of our young millwrights, Eric Ray, did a great job of helping me load it into the back of my Aerostar using a fork truck. The back end of the van was close to bottoming out from all the weight of that large box, but fortunately, it held up throughout the 250-mile trip up north. What else would I expect from that Ford Aerostar? It was a great van.

I had made that trip up north using Highway M-33 at the Rose City exit off of US-75 so many times in that van listening to oldies on the radio that I decided to write a poem as a tribute to my mentally challenged cousin, Rodney Huyck, who always wanted to be a disc jockey and loved listening to Golden Oldies.

Rodney was in his mid-fifties when he passed away, but not before leaving a lasting impression on the many people who knew and loved him.

Today with the way things are in the music industry, this poem could probably be made into a hit rap tune.

Rock'n Rodney

Cruis'n up highway M33
I was boogie'n thru one small town after another.
Rose City, Mio, Fairview and Cummin's
I was mov'n right out, man I was really humm'n.
Suddenly a familiar voice started com'n thru on the radio.
Yeah, it was the unmistakable sound of that famous Northern Michigan
D.J., Rock'n Rodney.
He was known for play'n some great golden oldie jams,
And today was no exception, Hot Damn.
Hotel California, Brown Sugar, Jump'n Jack Flash,
He had the graphic equalizer in my Aerostar, jumping up and down on
the dash.

Yeah, it was highway M-33, Rock'n Rodney and me,

mov'n thru the hills and trees.

As I drove on I couldn't help but get the feeling of being so free,

As I was getting closer and closer to Northern Michigan, USA.

Now what else can I say?

Crus'n up highway M-33

I was boogie'n thru one small town after another,

Rose City, Mio, Fairview and Cummin's

I was mov'n right out, man, I was really humm'n.

Before I knew it, I was thru Atlanta, and headed for Onaway,

where I'll be there to stay in Northern Michigan, USA.

Yeah, it was highway M-33, Rock'n Rodney and me,

Mov'n thru the hills and trees, Rock'n Rodney and me,

Mov'n thru the hills and trees, Rock'n Rodney and me,

Mov'n thru the hills and trees.

This book would not be complete if I did not say something about the last couple of days before I left the Rouge. The guys were really great about coming by and wishing me the best and congratulating me on being able to retire at the relatively young age of fifty-three.

Bill Geise, one of my longtime welder buddies, was almost in tears that last day, and like I joked about before, nothing ever comes easy when you're working with Bill Geise.

I also have to say thanks to fellow millwright, Billy Johnson, who definitely went out of his way to have people sign a going away card and collect over $500 from guys that I knew throughout the sprawling Rouge Complex. I will never forget that because I knew the considerable effort, he put into doing all of that running around. Thanks again, Bill, and best wishes to everyone at the Rouge.

Late in the summer of 2005, I received a phone call from a retired millwright buddy, Don, who is now living in the Naples, Florida area. Don obtained my phone number from my cousin, Mike Kowalski, who also lives in the Naples area and happened to be talking to Don one day.

Don was telling Mike that he was a retired Ford millwright from the Dearborn Rouge Complex and Mike said, "Hey, I have a cousin named Ralph Moore that was a millwright there too." Don almost fell over. He told Mike that he knew me and that we were friends since back in the mid-70's.

Don said that he was doing some carpenter work just to keep busy, and also that he had a health problem, asbestosis, second stage. When he told me this, I said, "Don remembers when we were apprentices working in the Power House and Pulverizer buildings? We used to patch up leaking coal dust holes in the duct work with a paste made from linseed oil and asbestos powder, and then when our hands became all nasty with coal dust, or worse yet, coal dust and grease mixed together, we would dip our hands in a cleaning solution that contained chemicals that were later banned." I said, "It's no wonder I can barely move my fingers some days because of arthritis caused not only from all the power tools and sledge hammers that we used, but also from those banned cleaning solutions that everyone used back in the '60's and '70's."

Before hanging up Don gave me a phone number to call, which I did and have since seen a doctor in regards to all of this and he determined that I was in the same boat as Don, asbestosis, second stage. Since that time, I have received some compensation from companies that have been held responsible for so many of these asbestos problems.

As I stated in the first edition of this book, I was hoping that this book might make a difference for some twenty or so guys who transferred over to Rouge Steel after December 1, 1989 when I did. We unfortunately ended up getting shafted because our local 600 maintenance and construction unit would not stand up for us by admitting they made a mistake. But they did make a mistake in not telling us that there was a fine print clause in the contract that would keep us from receiving a full Ford retirement, which is what they had promised us throughout the fall of 1989 and the winter and spring of 1990.

As I said before, our committeemen were constantly calling meetings and telling us that all we needed to get a full Ford retirement was sixty points or more, which was our age, plus our seniority at Ford, which we all had. If we had known that this was not true, absolutely none of us would have made the move to Rouge Steel.

We depended on and trusted them to tell us exactly the way things were and once again, unfortunately, they did not do this. Whether they were not aware of the fine print or not is probably debatable. All I know, is that none of them had the guts to stand up and back us on this issue. Sadly, what happened appears to be very similar to all the lies and cheating that many of the top UAW officers from various auto companies have gotten into hot water over in this last year, 2018. They ended up being charged for purchasing expensive clothing, jewelry, cars and homes, as well as taking luxury vacation trips from money stolen from various UAW funds.

So anyhow, they were practically begging us to transfer, and finally, Rouge Steel decided to up the ante and give us a bonus incentive to entice us to make this move. Never once was anything ever said about any stipulations. It was always, "If you have your sixty points, you don't have anything to worry about, you will have a full Ford retirement."

This duplicitous fiasco was similar to the one that our local 600 M/C unit botched years ago when they let all of the high seniority employees (who in 1973-74 signed off from ever returning to the Rouge when they left for greener pastures at the newly built Michigan Casting Center) come back to work in the Rouge with full seniority after Ford decided to shut it down in the early to mid-'80's.

This tricky little act is what forced most all of us lower seniority skilled tradesmen to end up on afternoons at Ford. They let these guys who nearly all went into the Steel Division, bump back into the Ford side when it was rumored that Ford was going to be selling this non-productive division. This bump was a regular procedure that could be done as long as it was during a standard two-week bumping period. If I remember correctly, there were two times a year that this could take place, once in the spring and once in the fall.

So once again, these guys made out like gangbusters no matter where they went. Obviously, it paid off for them to have, shall we say, "an uncle in the furniture business", because with the way our M/C unit took care of them, that's what it appeared to be. Mysteriously, the sheet they signed that said they would not be able to return to the Rouge, disappeared – how convenient. There was some sort of class-action lawsuit in regard to collusion in this case, but once again, the local 600's well connected unit came through unscathed.

I am not going to say any more about this except that our local 600 M/C should have been called on the carpet for that screw up and the one that cost us part of our retirement. I know this M/C unit, is or once was, one of the largest and most powerful units in the world, but what they did to us was wrong and they needed to make it right, but as of this date, it still hasn't happened.

The ultimate failure of our committeemen to stick up for us, has cost those of us who retired under their promises thousands of dollars in retirement benefits, and have forced some of the other guys to continue to work because they could not afford to retire with a Rouge Steel retirement package.

You can imagine how surprised and shocked one of our millwrights, Frank Williams, was when he decided to retire and was told he didn't have a full Ford retirement plan. Frank was a friendly black fellow about my size who had a slight stuttering problem, and when he found out about this he could hardly talk. He was in total shock, as were the rest of us once we heard about his unbelievable conversation.

When I retired a year later, I tried to set up a meeting with Jerry Sullivan, who was the local 600 president, but I could get no further than one of his top lieutenants. The guy just kept saying that there's nothing we can do for you or any of the others because it is stated right here in the contract that if you were not at Rouge Steel before such and such a date, you do not qualify for a full Ford retirement.

Local 600 always seems to be above wrong. All too often they get away with things that benefit them best, and this has a lot to do with their strong contacts with Ford Motor Company officials. They scratch each other's back, and it works very well for them. And, as I said, as of this date the back scratching hasn't ended.

I was hoping that my first book, Uncle Henry's Ford Rouge might make a difference once the word got out about all of this taking place, but so far no one has come forward and attempted to straighten this out and make things right. And, of course, after nearly twenty years, we all know there isn't a snowballs chance in hell that will ever happen – unfortunately.

A few years after the first book came out, I received a phone call from our friend Margo, who teaches law at Northern Michigan University in Marquette. She said something like, "Hey Ralph, how would you like to meet Mr. William Clay Ford Jr.? He is going to be giving a speech at the University during the day and then in the evening he will be doing the same thing at a dinner banquet in downtown Marquette." She called on a Saturday and said If I got up there Sunday, we would be able to catch his morning speech at the school on Monday. I, of course, agreed. We enjoyed the morning speech; however, it was the evening one that we were anxiously awaiting because Margo thought that I would probably have an excellent chance to meet Mr. Ford and hand him an autographed copy of the book.

And, she was right. We had to make our way around a few people and then patiently wait until he was through talking with some people. Finally, we were able to get through to him. I introduced myself and Margo, and then handed him a copy of my book as I explained to him how I came up with the name, Uncle Henry's Ford Rouge. He seemed genuinely interested in it and even had a little laugh about how I came up with the name. I knew we didn't have a lot of time, so I asked him if he didn't mind if Margo took a picture of us. He handed the book to his aid who was carrying a container to put things in that Mr. Ford received and then said, "no problem" and so she snapped the picture. It was so crowded in there that Margo wasn't able to step back very far for a good picture, but it still came out alright even though she was basically right in our face. We thanked him for letting us do this and then went to our seats to get ready for his speech.

We could easily see why he is so popular and in demand as a speaker. He has a very charismatic personality, and is completely at ease with his audience. I cannot remember exactly what he was talking about, but I'm pretty sure he mentioned something about the environment and how well his plan for the roof of the F150 truck plant is doing. As I mentioned earlier, he is very committed to seeing that the Rouge remains one of the worlds cleanest industrial plants in the world.

One other thing that has made this man and his family so enduring to the men and women of the Rouge is the fact that they genuinely care about their workers. When the explosion at the Power House happened, Bill Ford JR. was one of the first ones there and did all that he could to help out.

And, when GM and Chrysler filed for bankruptcy, the Fords chose to ride out the storm and came out smiling. This made the bond between the company and the workers even that much stronger.

So, thanks once again Mr. Ford and your family for giving us the opportunity to make a good life for our families. We deeply appreciate this and wish the company the best of luck in their pursuit of making the best cars and trucks in the world.

CHAPTER 20

Bonus Section

One of the perks from writing this amazing book has been that I have been able to meet and talk with a lot of really great people who have had ties to Ford Motor Company. I already mentioned the Chairman, William Clay Ford Jr., and I talked about working with Bob King when he was an electrician in the DSP.

Recently, while golfing with my buddy, Ken, at the UAW Black Lake Golf Course, we had just finished playing eighteen holes and were headed back to the clubhouse. As we came around the last turn, Ken, who works at this same UAW center, gave a shout out to a gray-haired guy who was sitting at an outdoor table. I asked him who that was and he said, "Dennis Williams". Knowing that he was the recently retired president of the UAW and that I had a few copies of my first book, "Uncle Henry's Ford Rouge", in the back seat of my F150, I rushed to the truck and quickly picked up and autographed a copy for him.

Fortunately, he was still there talking with a friend as I slowly walked towards their table. I smiled as I extended my hand and introduced myself as a retired skilled trades millwright from the Ford Dearborn Rouge Complex. I told him that after retiring I wrote this book about the Rouge. As I handed him the copy I had been carrying, he seemed genuinely pleased and said he was looking forward to checking it out.

As we conversed, I mentioned that I had worked with his predecessor, Bob King, in the DSP when we were both apprentices. I also mentioned that I was able to have a nice conversation with him one Sunday morning a few years ago while we were both attending Mass at St. Paul's Catholic Church in Onaway, where I am an usher. I told him that Bob agreed to have a couple pictures taken of the two of us standing in front of my Ford truck and wondered if he wouldn't mind if his friend took our picture. He smiled as he stood up, saying something like, "No problem". After the picture taking I asked him if it would be alright to use one of the pictures in the second edition of, "Uncle Henry's Ford Rouge". I explained to him that I was close to putting the finishing touches to the book and that hopefully, it would be ready in time for Christmas of this year, 2019. Before l left, he congratulated me on my latest effort with the book and said he would make sure to get a copy once it was out. I thanked him once again and then headed back to my truck.

Many of the people who purchased copies of Uncle Henrys Ford Rouge at some of my book signings were women who wanted to get a copy for their dad, grandfather, brother, or aunt and uncle who worked at one time or another in one of the Ford Plants. It seemed like they always had an interesting story to tell and I never got tired of hearing them. The seniors, especially, had a ton of questions to ask. They would want to know if I knew of someone such as, Harry Bennet, who was the head of Fords security back in the 1930's and was also known as the leader of the famous, Battle of the Overpass in 1937. I lust laugh when I get questions like that and explain to them that these people were way before my time and that I was only faintly familiar with them.

Once Henry II took over the reins of the company, he started making changes and one of the first things he did was to oust Bennet in 1945, the year I was born. Henry, "The Deuce" as he was known, was one of Edsel Fords three sons. Benson Ford and William Clay Ford, who was probably best known for being the long-time unsuccessful owner of our Detroit Lions, were the other two. So anyhow, because of all of these interesting questions by the seniors I was more or less forced to dig a little deeper into Ford's history.

Several years ago, my friend Margo gave me a book titled, Ford at Fifty and from this book I would like to share a few interesting lines. Remember this is before 1950. "The Ford Motor Company has changed too, from a one-room workshop to an industrial giant. One of its plants alone, the Rouge, could supply all the homes in Boston with electric power. It uses as much water as Detroit, Cincinnati, and Washington combined. It has 110 miles of railroad tracks, 22 Diesel locomotives, 81 miles of conveyors, and 4 bus lines."

This is a quote from Henry Ford in the same book. "I will build a motor car for the great multitude. It will be large enough for the family but small enough for individuals to run and care for. It will be constructed of the best materials, by the best men to be hired, after the simplest designs that modern engineering can devise. But it will be so low in price that no man making a good salary will be unable to own one – and enjoy with his family the blessings of hours of pleasure in God's great and open spaces."

And, these quotes from his Grandson, Henry II. "American industry should be a place of opportunity – a place in which men and women can grow and develop into better jobs." "We will never make a machine that cannot be substantially improved. We will never develop a technique that cannot be made substantially better. So long as search is encouraged, we will never come to the end of the road of progress."

Henry Ford II, The Deuce, was the most important person in the auto industry world for nearly forty years. He ended up saving his family's company from near bankruptcy and had a good time doing it while running the show. He was the main man and he proved it by firing two of the company's presidents. He was also married three times.

Some other executives I was asked about were guys like Lee Iacoca, who was best known for the development of the Ford Mustang and Pinto. This, of course, is before he left for Chrysler. Bunky Knudsen was another top executive who came to Ford from General Motors and eventually became president of the company in 1968. Then, there were always a lot of questions about Robert McNamara, whom Henry Ford II hired to help modernize the company in the late 1950's. In 1957, he was elected as the director of the company and then in 1960 he was named President. However, this was to be only a short stay because McNamara was a brilliant mind and eventually was chosen by President John F. Kennedy to serve as his Secretary of State.

Many of the people that I have spoken with either worked at the Rouge or had friends or relatives who did. Others, such as vendors, were in and out of the complex delivering products to the many different plants that made up the Rouge. A good deal of the guys that I have spoken with about the Rouge were sub-contractors coming and going throughout the years doing various jobs for the company. And the one thing they all seemed to have in common was that they were in awe of this truly amazing complex. It was the enormity of it all – it was like a city within a city.

The following stories are from some of the many letters and cards that I have received over the years since the first book came out. They just help add credibility to what I have been saying about many of the characters that we worked with and also in regards to how dangerous many of the jobs were and how our health was affected because of this.

This is from a guy who is probably close to eighty years old now. "What a great book! Your style of writing is great! I read close to $600.00 worth of books last year, so I'm probably as good of a judge as anybody, when it comes to judging the merits of an author. I messed up a disc real bad, while changing a hot blast valve on B furnace at age twenty-two. After that, I was laid up in bed for a week at Central Medical. After discharge I went on medical leave for a month. For many years I was laid up for a week every spring and every fall. My back got better when my own doctor put me on Meloxicam pills. Eventually, my records revealed that I had a ruptured disc."

I probably knew close to a dozen millwrights and welders and bosses that you mentioned. There were so many colorful characters! I was one of Zaya's journeymen. I loved the guy, but he was clumsy and negligent. I actually had to teach him how to operate a pair of channel locks!!!!!! His vision was so bad, it's no wonder that he was running people over with his kitty car when he was a boss in the DSP. PJ and I were going to Little Joe's one afternoon for lunch. It was raining cats and dogs! It was dark out. Visibility was very limited. We jumped in his car and took off and all of a sudden we came to a flying stop!! HE HIT A POLE IN THE PARKING LOT!!!! No disrespect intended but he was blind as a bat.

This same fellow told me that when he and Big Buck worked together on crane repair in the mill, Big Buck, who was about thirty pounds overweight and in his forty's, could still walk about ten feet ON HIS HANDS! One day the foreman addressed him as "Sunshine" and he thought Big Buck was going to throw the guy off that crane.

We were changing a truck on one of the cranes, over the Cold Mill I think. Somebody had hung a choker and a snatch block on the double angle that was on the bottom segment of the truss. We were wrapping up the job. Without anything to hang on to, Buck walked out on that double angle that was on the flat of course, bent down and unhooked the choker and grabbed the snatch block and turned around and walked back. I almost fainted. I said, 'Art, are you nuts?' He said, 'Naw man, that's my job.'"

There were some pretty rough people working on maintenance. Over lunch one day, in the blast furnace, these two guys, not tradesmen, both were Sicilians, were discussing the death of their previous boss. They were laughing and making a mockery of the whole thing. I guess the boss's name had been Obie. A bunch of guys had gone deer hunting together, up North. Obie was found dead, in the woods. He had been hit from behind with a blunt object. I had to stick my nose in. I asked if he was a pretty good boss. They were so lavish with their praises that the whole thing had "an odor" to it. Later on that day, my journeyman, a Romano, (an Italian from the mainland of Italy) called me aside. He said, "Why are you talking to these guys? They were members of the "Black Hand" during WWII! He further claimed the Black Hand had been the murder/extortion arm of the Mafia. I never talked to those guys again."

This is another story told to me during a recent phone call from my buddy Fred. He was actually told this story by one of the bosses in the DSP and it has to do with everyone's favorite Plant Engineering Manager Mr. Nunn. Nunn and two of his top Lieutenants were looking at an on-going project that was taking a little longer than Nunn would have preferred. It was at the north end of the plant by the bailer house during the cold months of winter. Nunn's one superintendent, Andy, is trying to explain that it was taking a lot of material and that it was quite cold outside. Nunn than says "Well God created all of this in seven days and your men can't even finish this in a couple months?" Andy just looks at him with a smile on his face and say's "well God didn't have you as his boss." Fred said it wasn't long after that, that Andy got demoted to General Foreman.

Another time involving Andy and Nunn again. During a discussion about a job, Andy got upset with Nunn's bull-crap and said something to him about being so damn pig headed. Shortly after this, once again, Andy gets demoted. Well, it turned out that this electrical foreman had a farm with some pigs on it. I'm not sure exactly how this happened, but I guess Nunn was heading to the salaried parking lot at the north end of the building and when he got close to where his car was parked, there was a pig's head lying close by. Amazing!! So, as you can see, it wasn't just the hourly workers that played games on each other. The stress got to everyone, and no-one was exempt from being humiliated when they screwed up.

CHAPTER 21

More Stories

To put the finishing touches to this book, I thought it would be interesting to get some stories from an ex Local 600 Tool and Die committeeman who goes by the same name as myself, Ralph. I have known Ralph for over ten years now as we both have an interest in sports, such as golf and senior pool league. Over these years, I have listened to some of his stories about the Rouge and found them rather interesting and humorous. So, I decided to set up a day where we could meet and discuss some stories about the Rouge from his perspective as a tool and die skilled tradesman and committeeman. And I am so glad that I did. He had some amazing stories to tell and not so real surprising was the fact that many of them were similar to what I have already mentioned. We were talking about the little scutters that foremen rode around on and he said that this one Sunday when it was rather quiet in the DSP, some of the tool & die guys to amuse themselves while on their break, would steal some of these little carts that weren't being used and ride around down in the basement and play tag while squirting each other with fire extinguisher water bottles held between their knees. They would try to spray water on the other guys cart to short circuit it and temporarily shut him down. Whoever was left standing was the winner. Anyhow, this one guy hit a pillar and fractured his ankle. So now they had to make up some kind of excuse in order to get him back on the job. They had been doing this for several weeks and so now this little escapade put a temporary damper on that. Whether alcohol was involved or not is probably debatable, but ——-.

He said pranks were big upstairs in the tool & die room, especially around the clay modeling area. They would make these little clay balls and put them in air guns that they used for their jobs and shoot them at each other. This was something that the men used to do in the tool & die building also. I always thought that those tool & die jobs were boring and I guess this rather confirms my suspicions. Amazing!! And I guess one of the reasons it was all so amazing was the fact that a lot of these guys were going out for their lunch on the weekend and often times some of the more serious drinkers would bring a pint or two back with them and by the end of the shift they could barely walk. They had to make sure they stayed away from heavy foot traffic as they went to punch out so as not to get caught staggering around. Hoorah!

Ralph said that he had spent a short time in the Frame plant and mentioned something that I had heard about before also, and that was about how big the many rats were over there. He said this one guy was taking a nap onetime and a rat ran right over his legs – yow! They actually brought a cat in to try and rid their self of some of those rats, but they were so huge that poor cat didn't stand a chance. They found it lying dead somewhere around the plant one day. Another time while over there he witnessed quite a knife fight between two brothers, who were actually good friends. Similar to what I witnessed while working in the old iron foundry as a young college student. He said everyone just backed off until one of the guys finally decided he had enough and that was the end of that. So, as you can easily see, there weren't too many dull moments no matter where you were working in the Rouge. Something was always going on that might catch your attention. Such as the time he saw a guy who was doing some arc welding on a frame line reach over and pick something up off of a frame. He took a hit on this big fat boy and set it back down on the frame to continue on down the line for whoever else might want to finish it off. It was something that was probably a daily occurrence.

We talked about how dangerous it was to work in the Rouge, and the fact that back in those days, it seemed like Fords was a little to lacks in their safety procedures. More often than not, it seemed that these things never caught anyone's attention until someone got seriously injured or even killed. And speaking of getting killed, no-one ever died in one of the plants, even though they actually did. That's right. They always were pronounced dead either on their way to the hospital or at the hospital. Just like the old guy who I saw die in the Glass Plant. The report came back saying that he died on his way to Oakwood Hospital. Once again, Amazing.

We continued to discuss some of the safety features that were there for the workers to use and ended up concluding that they cannot protect you if you don't use them. Unfortunately, too many guys have found this out after the fact. A good example is the die man in the DSP, who was in a hurry to finish up his job and failed to use the safety die blocks that were there to protect him from the machine accidentally cycling. It came down on his hand and stayed there until two guys managed to get on top of the die and manually back the press off his hand. By this time quite a few people had come to try and help. I guess there was a nurse standing by and when they finally got the die to go up enough to get his hand out, he turned white as a sheet and passed out in her arms. His hand had been severed right off.

Getting back on the humorous track again, Ralph was telling a story about this die maker in the DSP, who once had a serious accident that left him a little on the kooky side. I'm sure he was only kidding when he said this guy was President of the Eloise, Psychiatric Hospital. And, because he was a Mason, they took good care of him, which is what the Masons do. They look after each other. So, they found a job for him watching over the tool & die store they operated up there on the second floor. It was just a bunch of small stuff like candy, cookies, chips, and cigarettes. Anyhow, he had a brother who owned a tuxedo store and would give this guy old worn-out tuxedos. Well, he used to come into work all decked out in a fancy looking tux and then change into his coveralls. I guess the guy never drove a car, so he would take a bus home all dressed up like that, looking like some kind of big shot Whoo-Hoo!!

Man, those die makers were weird. I remember another guy like that up there that used to go around digging in the garbage and taking out whatever he felt he needed. It might be food or an old pair of shoes, it didn't matter if he saw it and liked it, he would haul it out and use it. Once again, amazing.

They definitely weren't afraid to get in trouble, that's for sure. They liked to have fun and weren't going to let anything stop them from doing that. One time during their lunch break, this one rich die maker who happened to own a cabin cruiser that was docked a short distance away on the Rouge River, brought his boat over to an area where some of the guys could get on board and go for a short cruise. True story! How they managed to get away with all these little games they played was truly amazing, but this was the Rouge and stories similar to this were not uncommon.

Before leaving the Elbo Bar near Canada Creek where we met, we talked about how often guys who were in a position to do so, would try to get away with using Ford material and labor to build things for their-selves or their buddies. One guy who was in a position to use a Ford credit card got caught doing this because of an audit that the company was doing. It was similar to what I mentioned earlier in the book about the foreman who used Ford labor and material to build his go cart business near the Irish Hills in Brooklyn, Mi. In the end, they usually get caught.

Finally, the last thing we talked about was the way things were handled when guys lost out on a full Ford retirement because of some miscommunication coming down from the higher up UAW big wigs to our committeemen. These committeemen might have misinformed us because it was possible that they did not know about the fine print in our contract when we left Ford's for Rouge Steel. Ralph said that if you were to follow the paper trail of those events it would more than likely lead right back to the very top. And, unfortunately, when things get that high up, there isn't much you can do about it. No-one is going to admit to screwing up. It is what it is, and that's just the way it's going to be.

Those days around the time I retired in 1998 were definitely history that will never be seen again. I wanted to show as close as possible how things really were. These are all true stories. Those were tough times for everyone involved and the men and women that survived were, for the most part, very adaptable and able to adjust to all of the many changes that were constantly being made and thrown at us. See my poem at the beginning of chapter 12, "We are the Men and Women of the Rouge."

The work, especially in Rouge Steel, was extremely dangerous and making it even worse was the fact that so many workers were walking around with sleep deprivation because of all the hours they had been working. That's right! Working anywhere from 80 to 113 hours a week for multiple weeks at a time could be brutal. It was tough on everyone involved including the home family life. Guys would start getting ornery, and hard to get along with. Tempers would flare up and all kinds of crazy things might happen. That's just the way it was and as I said before, those days like that were history that will never be seen again.

I want to conclude by saying thanks to everyone involved in this amazing story about life in the Rouge during this uncertain period of time from around 1965 to 1998. We had some good times and some tough times, but in the end, we were all survivors who made a good living for our families. And, as the late comedian and actor, Bob Hope would say, "Thanks for the memories".